This volume is based on a conference, *"Utraque Unum:* Individuality and Cooperative Action," held in Washington, D.C., on April 4 and 5, 1989, as part of the Bicentennial of Georgetown University. The conference was sponsored and supported by the University's Bicentennial Office; this book is one of a series of publications resulting from the Georgetown Bicentennial.

Publication of this series has been made possible in large part through a gift from Mrs. John R. Gaines. Her assistance and generosity is acknowledged with gratitude and appreciation.

INDIVIDUALITY
and
COOPERATIVE ACTION

Joseph E. Earley, *Editor*

Georgetown University Press / Washington, D.C.

Library of Congress Cataloging-in-Publication Date

Individuality and cooperative action / Joseph E. Earley, editor.
        p.   cm.
        1. Individualism. 2. Cooperation. 3. System theory. I. Earley.
Joseph E.
HM136.I46   1990   302.5′4--dc20   90-49576
ISBN 0-87840-516-X. -- ISBN 0-87840-517-8 (pbk.)

for Shirley

Every subject's duty is the King's;
but every subject's soul is his own.

W. Shakespeare, *King Henry V*, act 4, scene 2

CONTENTS

ACKNOWLEDGMENTS

I thank everyone who helped make the *Utraque Unum* conference a success, especially Mrs Kathleen Bayne and the other members of the Georgetown Chemistry Department staff; Rev. Charles L. Currie, S.J., Director of the University Bicentennial and his associates, particularly Dr. Kathleen Lesko; the *Utraque Unum* planning committee; and the students of Chemistry 042 (Spring, 1989).

J.E.E.

CONTRIBUTORS

Michael A. Arbib—Professor of Computer Science, Physiology, Electrical Engineering and Psychology, Director of the Center for Neural Engineering, The University of Southern California; author of *Vision, Brain and Cooperative Computation*and coauthor of *The Construction of Reality* (1983 Gifford Lectures).

Murray Bowen—Clinical Professor of Psychiatry, Director of The Family Center, Georgetown University Medical Center; originator of Bowen Family Systems Theory; coauthor of *Family Evaluation*. Professor Bowen died in October, 1990.

Louis Dupré—T. Lawrason Riggs Professor of Religious Studies, Yale University; author of *Marx's Social Critique of Culture* and *The Deeper Life, A Meditation on Christian Mysticism*.

Joseph E. Earley—Professor and, until July 1, 1990, Chairman, Department of Chemistry, Georgetown University; author of articles and reviews on chemical reaction mechanisms and on process philosophy.

Frederick Ferré—Research Professor of Philosophy, The University of Georgia; author of *The Philosophy of Technology* and *God and Global Justice*.

O. B. Hardison, Jr.—University Professor of English, Georgetown University; author of *Entering the Maze: Identity and Change in Modern Culture* and *Disappearing through the Skylight: Identity in a Technological Culture*. Professor Hardison died in August, 1990.

Monika K. Hellwig—Professor of Theology, Georgetown University; author of *Death and Christian Hope* and *Christian Women in a Troubled World*.

Ivor Leclerc—E. Fuller Callaway Professor of Metaphysics and Moral Philosophy, Emory University; author of *The Nature of Physical Existence* and *The Philosophy of Nature*.

Howard Margolis—Department of Public Policy Studies, The University of Chicago; author of *Patterns, Thinking and Cognition* and *Selfishness, Altruism and Rationality*.

Mancur Olson—Distinguished Professor of Economics, The University of Maryland; author of *The Logic of Cooperative Action* and *The Decline of Nations*.

Arthur R. Peacocke—Oxford University; author of *Introduction to the Physical Chemistry of Biological Organization* and *God and the New Biology*; priest of the Church of England, Warden of the Order of Ordained Scientists (O.O.S.).

William M. Sullivan—Professor of Philosophy, LaSalle College; coauthor of *Habits of the Heart*, author of *Reconstructing Public Policy*.

Edward O. Wilson—Frank S. Baird Professor of Science, Harvard University; author of *Sociobiology*, of *Genes, Mind and Culture* and of *The Ants*.

James A. Yorke—Director of the Center for Physical Science and Technology and Research Professor of Mathematics, The University of Maryland; author of many papers and reviews on the mathematics of chaos and on nonlinear dynamics.

Louise B. Young—Science writer; author of *The Unfinished Universe* and *The Blue Planet*.

1

INTRODUCTION:

INDIVIDUALITY AND COOPERATIVE ACTION

Joseph E. Earley

A central intellectual concern of our time is finding a new basis for understanding the relationship between group action and individual integrity, in many contexts. Until recently, relationships involving groups and individuals were dealt with using concepts and attitudes that gained general acceptance during the "scientific revolution" of three centuries ago. The rise of individualism in social theory and practice is related to the success of mechanistic physics and corpuscular chemistry in explaining natural phenomena using analysis to ultimate constituents (atoms). In recent years, attention has been called to limitations of some of the main concepts that derive from the scientific revolution. Humanists have concluded that radical individualism has pernicious consequences, and scientists who have explored self-organizing physical systems have suggested that physical science itself needs to rethink some long-held assumptions.[1]

    This book is composed of essays by scholars in a wide variety of disciplines dealing with how autonomous units (atoms, neurons, organisms, persons, societies) spontaneously develop and maintain patterns of coherent coordinated activity, and on the consequences for general culture of these and related questions. These essays are based on papers presented at a conference, "*Utraque Unum*: Individuality and Cooperative Action," held at Georgetown University in Washington, D.C. on April 4 and 5, 1989 supported and sponsored by the Bicentennial of the University. *Utraque Unum*, roughly translated as "one from the two," is the motto of Georgetown University. It is traditionally taken to mean that one of the University's main goals is to achieve coherence between science and liberal scholarship, on the one hand, and the moral and religious traditions in which the University stands, on the other hand. The conference and this book are intended to contribute to that integrative aim.

Each chapter after this one consists of a longer paper and a shorter one. In some cases the shorter paper is a response to the longer one; more frequently, the shorter paper develops a point of view that is different from but more or less related to the main thrust of the longer paper. A few of the chapters include some discussion involving other participants of the conference. The first paper is concerned with aspects of the present human situation in a world increasingly influenced by technological developments. Subsequent papers explore the impact of new scientific understanding of cooperative behavior of complex systems on widely held philosophical presuppositions. Later papers consider the importance of questions of human individuality and group cohesion for humanity's future. In the final chapter, a lively discussion involving most of the main contributors and other participants summarizes and extends the interdisciplinary dialog.

*   *   *

Human use of tools is ancient indeed, but intimate association of people with machines, particularly complex ones, has become common only relatively recently . In chapter 2, O.B. Hardison, Jr. considers metaphors of machine life and of machine evolution as they are connected with contemporary perceptions of computers, by scientists and by others. Alan Turing's 1950 prediction that by the end of the twentieth century "the use of words and generally educated opinion will have altered so much that one will be able to speak of machines thinking without expecting to be contradicted" seems likely to be correct. The many man-machine interactions that characterize modern life have changed how we speak, how we think, and what we consider to be characteristically human. Rapid progress of computer technology, such as the invention of "neural networks," has caused metaphors that once seemed extreme to become commonplace and has blurred the distinction between the human and the mechanical. There are even intimations of a "disappearance of the human," as people and computers become ever more closely integrated.

James A. Yorke gives a specific example of how computer-based mathematical studies of quite simple physical systems have altered our understanding of science and of knowledge. Simulations of the motion of a pendulum, governed by clear and deterministic equations, often yield results that are best described as "chaos." Chaos-generating systems are neither rare nor unusual; rather, it is the exactly solvable problems traditionally discussed by scientists that are exceptional. The notion that the universe works in inexorable, predetermined ways, as was suggested by the mechanical philosophy of the seventeenth century and as has been a tacit presupposition of modern culture, is now quite untenable.

*   *   *

"Life is self-assembling," Edward O. Wilson writes in the third chapter. Scientists generally agree that biological organisms, including humans, have come into existence through "largely autonomous" processes, although this seems contrary to "the traditional religious viewpoint." Resolution of the tension between "scientific" and "religious" outlooks must involve examination of the origin of human nature in biological evolution. Human capabilities and also human culture are biologically constrained in important and specific ways. Social animals (sponges, ants, termites, etc.) have been outstandingly successful. The imperfect but effective human propensity for purposeful collective action has enabled mankind to reach and maintain a large and widespread population, but current human practices (such as destruction of tropical rain forests) are bringing extinction to many species, and may well threaten the survival of humanity itself.

Louise Young points out that self-organization has occurred repeatedly in the evolution of the cösmos; submicroscopic particles unite into atoms—atoms form molecules—galaxies, stars and planets coalesce from clouds of molecular hydrogen—life emerges in primeval oceans-complex animals develop-human societies flourish. She notes that "the individual units of each level act as the building-blocks for the next higher level of complexity and, therefore, at each stage the system is built of larger, more complex entities, and each stage opens up a new range of potentialities....In general when units converge to form a larger whole, the integrity of the individual units is not sacrificed."

*   *   *

In chapter 4, Michael A. Arbib considers how "interactions among multitudes of units yield properties that are absent when those units are considered in isolation." He gives examples of such emergence at several levels of complexity. For instance, individual atoms in a bar of iron are tiny magnets, each with a magnetic axis pointing in some direction. Usually, the individual magnetic atoms are randomly aligned, so that the entire bar has no overall magnetization. But if a nonmagnetized bar is placed in a strong external magnetic field, most of the atoms eventually become aligned in the same direction, and the bar of iron itself becomes a magnet. Magnetization of the bar is not lost if the external magnetic field is turned off, because the pull of neighboring (aligned) atoms influences each individual atom to maintain the common alignment. As a second example, computer routines (algorithms) that model the functioning of visual neurons indicate that important similarities exist between cooperative action of neurons in processing information and interactions of atomic magnets to produce magnetized iron bars. The signal produced by a particular neuron must be integrated with those produced by many other neurons. This is done by repeatedly interpreting signals from one or a few neurons in terms of signals from other groups of neurons. As part of each such computation, prior interpretations for each neuron are modified on the basis of the interactions of the other neuron-groups. Eventually, a single overall result that is consistent with all of the individual signals is obtained. The interpretation of the signal from any particular neuron depends on the interaction of all the other neurons (as the alignment of a particular magnetic atom is influenced by the alignment of other atoms in its neighborhood).

Analogous interactive processes involving large groups of neurons give rise to "schemas" ("'units' of mind") that are involved in the more complicated activities of brains. Schemas are subject to mutual interaction and to external influences in ways that are analogous to the two simpler cases (magnetic atoms and neurons). In the case of humans, a unique set of schemas constitutes the "personality" of each individual. A particular human social group is defined by complex sets of schemas (language, religion, ideology, science, etc.) held in common by the members of that group. Those schemas are maintained, and passed from generation to generation, through cooperative interactions and external influences, analogous to those that exist on less complex levels.

Murray Bowen sketches the "family systems theory" that has been developed in his psychiatric clinic and research. Families work best when each member functions as an independent self, but the development of each individual as a self ("differentiation") requires a well-functioning family emotional system. Clinical symptoms can often be understood, and treated, on the basis of family structures that involve inadequate differentiation of family members. A considerable degree of family integration is usually necessary for development of effective human individuality.

*   *   *

Arthur R. Peacocke begins his paper (chapter 5) with an evocation of the profound shock that educated people felt when ideas connected with the rise of science displaced medieval cosmology. He then briefly summarizes some concepts that have characterized science "until the middle of this century," including "the criterion of predictability as that which characterized successful science and a view of the world of nature as mechanistic and deterministic." But the type of mathematical result that James Yorke discussed in chapter 3, and other features of complex nonlinear dynamic systems that are studied by chemists and by other scientists, require a radically different view of nature and of science. Nature is no longer seen primarily as an array of composite entities (organisms, cells, molecules, atoms, elementary particles,...) with the behavior of each determined by the properties of the "lower-level" components; now a "'top-down' causative influence of the system on its components" is also widely recognized. Both the emergence of life and the existence of human self-determination were highly problematic in the earlier mechanistic view; the new outlook is more congenial for understanding both biological and human emergence. But the new approach may differ in important ways from the cosmology that has prevailed in the recent past, as that world view differed from earlier ones.

Ivor Leclerc points out that Newton's conception of the ultimate physical individual as "a particle of matter, a body *per se*," was a major departure from prior natural philosophy, but that idea has become so deeply embedded in modern thought that it still persists as an unquestioned premise. Developments in science, including some mentioned in this volume, have shown that this concept is not generally applicable, and that some of its implications are not correct. He suggests an alternative concept—that the fundamental characteristic of physical individuals is *relational acting*.

*   *   *

In chapter 6, Mancur Olson observes that both morals and incentives are needed to make societies work well, and both are found in every culture. Morals alone are *not* sufficient for a community to prosper, a structure of incentives is also necessary. Many aspects of human social organizations can be understood in terms of the action of rational individual agents, operating under various incentives. For instance, the preference of rural Chinese for rule by *stationary* warlords, and aspects of the behavior of such rulers towards their subjects, can be understood on that basis. Detailed consideration of how incentives work can suggest improved arrangements. For instance, if the organization and structure of American political parties were strengthened, responsibility for the results of policies could be assigned more readily, and generally beneficial action by politicians would be more likely. Morality must be relied on when no structure of incentives can be devised to motivate necessary action, but effective incentives should be preferred to moral suasion whenever possible.

Howard Margolis argues for a somewhat different understanding of the relation between self-interest and social (moral) motivation. *Both* self-interest and social motivation are generally involved in human action, just as prices are determined by both supply and demand. Adequate social theory ought to take both sorts of motivation explicitly into account from the start, rather than doing its analysis on the basis of self-interest alone (insofar as that is possible), including moral motivation only as an adjustment.

*   *   *

According to Louis Dupré (chapter 7), Greeks and Romans of the classical period, and also Jews and early Christians, held that meaning and purpose were *given in* nature; that the goal of life was finding one's proper place in the cosmos. After the early Renaissance, the alternative concept that man had no fixed nature came into prominence, and the goal of life became "to define humanity independently of any 'given' place." This shift brought about a separation between culture and nature and led to unprecedented emphasis on *the self* as source of meaning and value. These attitudes prepared the way for the origin and growth of modern science, and for the subsequent development of technology and large-scale industrial society. Philosophy articulated new views of nature and of humanity. Art, too, was profoundly changed, and became a means of self-expression, independent of any religious or moral justification. The result of the "turn toward the self" was eventually to empty the self of meaning and value and produce a fragmented, incoherent universe. Returning to ideas of the past is not possible, the solution to excessive self-centeredness must be through developing "inwardness" of an appropriate sort. What is needed is "an attitude in which transcendence can be recognized again," so that freedom may be recovered by "detachment from the merely objective."

William M. Sullivan concurs in the diagnosis, but prescribes a different treatment. He suggests that what should be cultivated is, as Hegel urged, "participation in institutional and cultural life ... in a manner appropriate to modern subjectivity," that is, participation "freely chosen and consciously shaped." The interconnectedness of all human activities and the interdependence of the world's peoples are now apparent. Ecological concern has moved from a peripheral to a central position. "Awareness that we are inextricably involved in a natural order which transcends our attempts to understand and control it are being forced on us by our very attempts to extend our subjective will to dominate."

*   *   *

Monika Hellwig (chapter 8) maintains that "the urgent questions of human survival and well-being" involve "the shaping of values, of goals, of personal and social decisions and of real commitments." Judeo-Christian tradition, properly understood, can provide a basis for achieving this. The Creation stories of the Bible assert that meaning is given in the constitution of reality and that human persons and communities are *within* the creative process. "Human beings are called forth to be in the likeness of the Creator, themselves in some sense creative, spontaneous, self-defining, autonomous; a drive in the direction of autonomy, self-definition and world-definition is constitutive of their very being." But human freedom and autonomy is conditioned, dependent on "not putting the self at the center, for the self is incapable of sustaining that position... True human freedom is reached finally as a communal freedom—not collective but communal—dependent on networks of interdependence...ultimately grounded in a source that transcends them." The biblical story of the tree in the garden can be understood as signifying that prior human decisions, as well as the initial creation, set conditions on community-building. Christianity has a "radical conviction about transformations seen as moving to a purposeful end." Scientific and technological developments can contribute to, or hinder, "the maturing of human autonomy into authentic patterns of solidarity." This becomes clear in the economic development of the Third World; technical power must be channeled so as "to serve authentic interaction of responsible persons growing towards responsible and voluntary solidarity."

Every technology involves both value-meanings and knowledge-meanings, writes Fred Ferré. Technology is "constantly alive with human wants and human capabilities," but those values are not always laudable, and those capabilities are sometimes used perniciously. As Professor Hellwig has urged, technologies must be evaluated in terms of whether they contribute to "authentic patterns of solidarity"—but that solidarity must extend beyond humanity and include the rest of nature. In order to form the basis of the ethic, an environmental one, that is now needed, biblical narrative and Christian anthropology must be understood in ways that are not excessively anthropocentric.

*   *   *

Questions from the floor, and discussion between the main contributors, are included in chapter 9. In some cases questions and discussion clarified points made originally, but divergences between points of view were also sharpened. The scientists were in agreement about self-organization in physical, chemical, biological and neuronal systems, and that recent progress in these areas represents a major change from prior scientific approaches. Also, all agreed that there are situations in which the interests of humanity at large may be endangered by applications of technology (including both advanced and crude versions). It was suggested that self-organization of natural systems contradicts the concept of divine creation but a general consensus developed that the science of interest here is consistent either with theistic or with atheistic interpretations. There was also general agreement that the development of an explicit notion of the autonomy of the human individual has been a major achievement of modernity, and that any adequate future social arrangements must take that autonomy fully into account. But full human individuality must be achieved by each person within a societal context; there are strong and reciprocal influences between individuals and families, religious groups, political and economic instutions and cultures. The networks of interrelationship that sustain and replicate these social entities must be valued along with individual persons.

*   *   *

"Self-organization" occurs on astronomical, physical, chemical, biological and psychological levels. The Newtonian principle that "matter" *per se* is inert and moves only under external influences is now seen to be incomplete; natural systems exhibit *intrinsic* propensities for action and structuring. Renaissance humanists ascribed self-determination to human persons; analogous capacities are now seen as being general characteristics of nature. The "self-centered" culture derived intellectual support from the success of corpuscular science; the new sciences of self-organization[1] may foster quite different outlooks.

Coherent patterns arise spontaneously in natural systems (Figure 1.1). Is it likely that networks of association that emerge in human

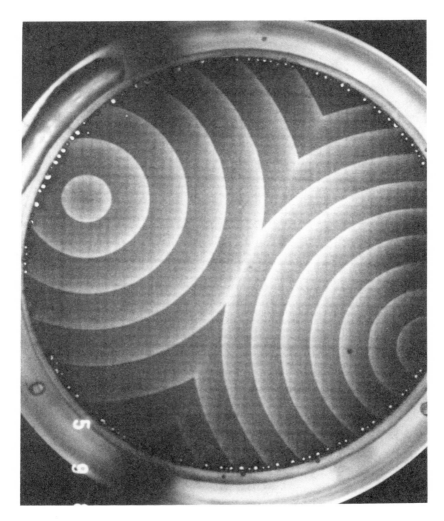

Figure 1.1 Pattern spontaneously developed when a 0.5 mm layer of solution containing bromate ion, malonic acid, and ceric ion in dilute sulfuric acid is placed in contact with a layer of cation-exchange resin containing ferroin indicator. Photo courtesy of Prof. Kenneth Showalter of the University of West Virginia.[4]

affairs are somehow related to the self-organization of other natural systems? Clearly, human culture has a biological basis, but complex sets of concepts, ideas and practices (including languages, religions, sciences, moralities, technologies) are of major importance in human life and development. Social relationships and social cognition play important parts in the behavior of our primate relatives, apes and baboons;[2] in human societies, technological practices greatly influence reproductive success and strongly affect the propagation of languages, cultures and ideologies. Recent research indicates that Indo-European language and culture spread as a result of the population growth made possible by the discovery of agriculture[3]. This may be considered "top-down" causation; technological innovation brought about major shifts in the makeup of human populations and therefore may be said to have "caused" large changes in the human gene-pool.

The behavior patterns that are characteristic of humanity continually and quite rapidly change, under the influence of both natural and technological environments. The evolution of the cosmos has been characterized by repeated coalescence of units into larger aggregates that then join to make yet more complex entities; new sorts of coherence are now emerging from the growing global interconnectedness of mankind.

Future social structures will have to combine effective respect for the autonomy of individual human persons with forceful concern for preservation and enhancement of local and global environments. If environmental sensitivity were to be lacking, the biological survival of the human species would be doubtful; without personal self-determination, individual human development would be stunted and long-term social stability unlikely. Achieving coherence of these two features, although difficult, is necessary for human survival and flourishing. But it is not true that whatever is necessary for species persistence does in fact occur. People do not generally organize for cooperative action merely because there is a job that needs to be done, for the general benefit.[5] Individual commitment to socially useful cooperative action does not appear just because it is needed.

Human motivations have always involved both incentives and morals, and both kinds of stimulus have historically been connected to religious narrative and practice. Biological evolutionary advance usually occurs when a preexisting structure takes on new functions (lungs developed out of the esophagus, for instance).[6] Similarly, preexisting social structures, formerly having different functions, can develop in ways that meet new needs. It has been reported[7] that, in prehistory, Ionian Greeks responded to unsettling effects of the growth of relatively large towns, and of the origin of widespread trade, by developing modified religious ideas that guided behavior in new ways; these concepts were then spread throughout the Greek-speaking world through the epic poetry of Homer. In the unstable world of the later Roman Empire, the sense of the dignity and worth of the individual that was offered by Christianity was a major factor in the spread of that religion;[8] in the following centuries, coherent policies of the Roman Church weakened the influence of extended families, preparing the social ground for the individualism of Renaissance humanism.[9] Evolutionary development of religious consciousness and practice has been one of humanity's most successful ways of dealing with change.

Large-scale social structures that evolve in the future, if they are to function successfully, will need to incorporate aspects drawn both from science and from previously existing religious traditions. Widespread and numerous human populations cannot be sustained without the detailed knowledge of natural systems that has been gained through science. Similarly, the attitudes and tendencies that make modern life, and science, possible are connected in complex ways with prior traditions. Every scientist knows that present science is deficient in important respects; religious people recognize that there are problematic aspects of past and present religious systems, and also with their practice. Religions that celebrate nature have frequently been careless of individual lives and values; individualistic religious and political systems have often contributed to environmental degradation; socialist ideologies and religions of harmony have managed to combine both of these bad effects.[10]

Newtonian physics, the chemical periodic table, and similar scientific results are recognized as major human cultural accomplishments. The doctrine of the value of the individual human person, as developed by patristic Christianity and by Renaissance humanism, is also a precious achievement. Although scientific concepts and techniques and also religious ideas and practices will themselves be undergoing continual evolutionary development,[11] future social institutions must prize both sorts of value, and continually strive to attain coherence between them.

Nature abounds in examples of complex coordinated activity deriving from interactions of relatively simple units. The details of interactions that give rise to auto-patterning differ at each level of organization (astronomical, physical, chemical, biological, neural, etc.). The special characteristic that pertains to human organizations is that cooperative action is not brought about only by mindless forces but rather by conscious decisions of rational agents. Great benefits have been realized from the degree of conscious cooperation that has thus far occurred, but by comparison with other natural systems,[12] these arrangements are relatively crude. Collective human action on a grand scale will be needed in the future, and it must emerge from free decisions of autonomous persons. It will be evolutionarily necessary that men and women count a collective gain as an individual benefit, and that societies foster development of the individuality of their members. This will not occur without social and institutional arrangements that take account of both the achievements of science *and* the values of evolved traditions.

REFERENCES

1. Gregoire Nicolis and Ilya Prigogine, *Exploring Complexity* (New York: Freeman 1989); Ilya Prigogine, *Being and Becoming, Time and Complexity in the Physical Sciences* (New York: Freeman 1980); Ilya Prigogine and Isabelle Stengers, *Order Out of Chaos, Man's New Dialogue with Nature* (New York: Bantam 1984); David Pines, ed. *Emerging Syntheses in Science* (New York: Addison Wesley, 1988); Hermann Haken, *Information and Self-Organization* (New York: Springer, 1988).

2. The experiment is described in the *Journal of Physical Chemistry 93* (6 April 1989), 2774.

3. Dorothy Cheney, Robert Seyfarth, and Barbara Smuts, "Social Relationships and Social Cognition in Nonhuman Primates," *Science* 234 (12 December 1986), 1361-66.

4. Colin Renfrew, *"Archaeology and Language: The Puzzle of Indo-European Origins* (Cambridge: Cambridge University Press, 1988); "The Origins of Indo-European Languages," *Scientific American* 261 (October 1989), 106-14.

5. Mancur Olson, *The Logic of Collective Action* (Cambridge, Mass.: Harvard University Press, 1965).

6. Gregory T. Alles, "Wrath and Persuasion: The Iliad and Its Contexts" *Journal of Religion* 70 (April 1990), 167-81.

7. François Jacob, "Evolution and Tinkering," *Science* 196 (10 June 1977), 1161-66.

8. Michael Mann, *The Sources of Social Power* (Cambridge: Cambridge University Press, 1986).

9. Jack Goody, *The Development of the Family and Marriage in Europe* (Cambridge: Cambridge University Press, 1983).

10. Yi-Fu Tuan, "Our Treatment of the Environment in Ideal and Actuality," *American Scientist* 58 (May-June 1970), 246-49.

11. E.g. David R. Peel, "Is Schubert M. Ogden's God Christian?" *Journal of Religion* 70 (April 1990), 147-66.

12. Jeffrey Dean, Daniel J. Aneshansley, Harold E. Edgerton, and Thomas Eisner, "Defensive Spray of the Bombardier Beetle: A Biological Pulse Jet," *Science* 248 (8 June 1990), 1219-22.

2 : 1

MACHINES, METAPHORS,
AND HORIZONS OF INVISIBILITY*

O. B. Hardison, Jr.

> The machine that repeats
> Its movement without faltering
> Is as simple as the child
> Who repeats his prayer
>   —Franz Hellens, *"Simplicité"*

My subject in this essay is machines—most especially comput-ers—and metaphors. It is a theme explicitly announced in my epi-graph, which is taken from the collection *Eclairages* published in 1926 by the French avant-garde poet Franz Hellens. The fact that the epigraph is from the work of a poet is not an accident. The so-called "discovery of the machine" is a major theme of European art and lit-erature between 1900 and 1930. It is a cultural response to the enor-mous increase in the frequency and what might be called the depth of everyday transactions between man and machine that took place in the early twentieth century. The themes evident in the poetry of Hellens are also evident in the poetry of Apollinaire, the art of Marcel Duchamp and Francis Picabia, the sculpture of Jean Arp, and the ar-chitectural program of the Bauhaus. They can be traced in American art and literature in, for example, the poetry of Hart Crane and Carl Sandburg and in the painting of Joseph Stella.

---

*This essay is developed from the final section of Dr. Hardison's *Disappear-ing through The Skylight: Culture and Technology in the Twentieth Century* (Viking/Penguin, 1989), with special emphasis on the metaphorics—and thus the phenomenology—of the rapidly developing cultural symbiosis between humans and intelligent or quasi-intelligent machines.—Ed.

My object here is to examine what is, I think, a striking extension of these themes that is occurring today in the wake of the emergence of what seem to many—including many of their developers—to be new types of machines, machines that exhibit some form of human intelligence. Since both the development of these machines and much of the commentary that I will examine seems to belong in the domain of science rather than the humanities, I should state at the beginning that I approach it from the point of view of a humanist, which I am, rather than a scientist, which I am not, although I confess to being an admirer of both the results and the elegant methods of the sciences to which I will refer. In accord with this focus, I will not be discussing machines *per se*, but the perceptions that people, including scientists, have of them, and, in particular, perceptions embodied in two metaphors—the metaphor of machine life and the metaphor of machine evolution.

Here a further qualification must be added. Throughout the entire range of discussion of the subject, there seems to be a fundamental ambivalence about the meaning assigned to the word "intelligence." "Intelligence" can mean merely the ability to do easily and quickly certain tasks that are onerous for humans. Well before the twentieth century machines were developed that exhibited this sort of intelligence, but it is obvious that so-called "smart machines" exhibit it in larger quantities and in far more spectacular ways than their predecessors. However, as machines have gotten smarter and as discussion of their abilities has ramified, it has become apparent that those who use the term "intelligence" mean something more than the ability to calculate rapidly or to solve complex equations or even to reason logically and play games like chess. In current discussions of machine intelligence, "intelligence" is almost always identified with specifically human qualities, although the qualities are usually implied rather than directly described. Evidently, the real, if usually unstated, subject is whether machines are developing abilities like those of complex living organisms.

Ultimately, the question is not whether machines are smart but whether they can enter into discourse with humans on something like an equal basis, which means whether they can be regarded as having something like self-awareness or consciousness. This meaning is implicit in the so-called "Turing Test" for machine intelligence. The Turing Test comes at the very dawn of the age of smart machines— 1950—and references to it recur throughout the later literature on the subject. We will return to it later, but for the moment what I want to stress is that it does not measure intelligence in the sense of cleverness, but the ability of a machine to behave in such a way that it cannot be distinguished from a human agent by someone in communication with it. Thus, to speak of "the metaphor of machine intelligence" is really to speak of a metaphor of machine consciousness.

Note, however, that the metaphor is, at this point, emphatically a metaphor. To use it in this way is not to imply that machines are (or can be) conscious in a literal sense, any more than to say that "my love is like a red, red rose" is to mean that my love has leaves growing on her legs and is covered with brambles. A metaphor is metaphorical precisely because it is *not* taken literally. The metaphor of machine intelligence or consciousness implies merely that in some circumstances and from some points of view, machines exhibit characteristics that are usually associated with the behavior of conscious agents or that are thought to be elements essential to the possibility of conscious or conscious-appearing behavior.

I suspect that the tendency of those who argue about the nature of machine processes to speak in terms of "intelligence" rather than "consciousness" is partly because "intelligence" sounds more objective and "definable"—perhaps more "scientific"—than "consciousness." This is not, however, to deny the ambiguity implicit in several references that will be encountered below to "machine intelligence." It is, rather, to call attention to the ambiguity and to warn the reader that, although I may offer one interpretation of a given comment, other interpretations are not only possible but might be preferred by another reader. At any rate, whatever the reader may conclude about a given passage, the word "intelligence" cannot be taken for granted but must be interpreted whenever it appears in discussions of smart machines.

I will not concern myself initially with specific instances of metaphors attributing life and evolution to machines but will focus on something that seems to me to be important for understanding the context of such metaphors. Although explicit concern with the relations between men and machines is a major cultural theme of the twentieth century for reasons already noted, metaphors attributing life and intelligent design to things that are inanimate are ancient and are found so widely in early cultures that they can be called archetypal. That helps to explain why many apparently current metaphors of machine life have a familiar feeling about them, even though the subjects to which they explicitly refer were unknown before the twentieth century. If this is true-if the root metaphors that we are concerned with here are, indeed, archetypal-then the emergence of life-like machines in the later twentieth century cannot be viewed as an entirely new historical development but is in some sense a realization-or at least a decisive advancement-of a project that first announces itself at a very early stage in the development of human culture and may, in fact, be inseparably associated with the moment when human consciousness differentiates itself from a surrounding "other" that is conceptualized as being complementary to the self and therefore saturated with human intentionality.

Whatever one concludes about the archetypal aspect of metaphors of machine life and intelligence, the increasingly frequent use of such metaphors both in everyday speech and in serious scientific and philosophical debate reflects a symbiosis between man and machine that is increasingly deep and increasingly pervasive in modern culture.

In view of this symbiosis, two conclusions seem valid. First, it would seem that man and machine can no longer be thought of as separate in quite the old way. Today the human environment is understood in terms of knowledge made possible by machines and shaped by powers that are only available because of machines. This means that machines are already incorporated in the deep structure of modern consciousness. Where does man stop and machine begin? Given the depth of the interrelation, does it make sense to pose this question in this way?

This leads to a second problem. That is, if the relation between man and machine is already so deep that it is difficult to draw a line between them, does this fact weaken the metaphoric nature of metaphors of machine life? Put the idea another way. Metaphors are only metaphors when they are understood as such. For example, the word "target" comes from the Latin for "shield" (*targus*). "Target" was originally a metaphor-a target was "like" a shield because it was intended to be shot at. In modern English, however, "target" is no longer a metaphor because almost no one who uses it thinks of it in relation to its etymology. Instead, it is simply the name for a thing that exists in the world. On the other hand, to "set a target for production" *is* still metaphoric because "target" is clearly and unambiguously associated in modern English with shooting rather than manufacturing. To apply this observation to the current subject, if no clear line can be drawn in modern culture between man and machine, does this not undercut one's instinctive and common-sense assurance that the metaphor of machine life is, indeed, metaphoric? And if this is true at present, is it not a significant question whether what seem to be obvious metaphors of machine life to the present generation will continue to seem metaphorical for the foreseeable future?

*   *   *

As already noted, the metaphor of machine life has a long prehistory that helps to explain its perennial fascination. It probably goes back ultimately to the feeling—apparently universal among primitive peoples—that man shares the earth with intelligent nonhuman beings, some of them benign and some terrifyingly destructive. This is the source of the gods and daemons that so richly populate the early mythologies of every human culture.

These beings are not initially understood as machines, but they are understood as responsive to human control because they can be evoked or summoned up or propitiated or avoided by specific actions and incantations.

The idea of benign nonhuman companions is objectified in more developed cultures by mechanical automata, which have exercised a continuous fascination from ancient times to the present. Golden mechanical men were said by the Greeks to have assisted Hephaestos at his forge. Later still, a wonderful cross-section of the mechanical gadgets and toys that were known in antiquity is provided by the two treatises of Hero of Alexandria, probably dating from the fourth century A.D., on automata and pneumatic devices. After the invention of the escapement mechanism in the late Middle Ages, clockwork figures began to populate the spires of Europe's cathedrals and town halls. In the eighteenth century, sophisticated mannequins wrote letters with quill pens and played (or seemed to play) musical instruments. The twentieth century has seen a veritable population explosion of wind-up and battery-operated vehicles, animals, mannequins, and toy robots.

Charming, you say. But the tradition also has a dark side. The primitive world is peopled with daemons as well as kindly gods, and both Zeus and Jehovah can be figures of terror as well as loving fathers of humanity. Mythology is littered with beings—and machines—that, once invented, got out of control. The legend of the Golem tells of a rabbi who created an artificial creature to protect the Jews of Prague. The Golem soon turned violently against its masters and had to be destroyed. This legend is of special interest because it is one of the sources of Mary Shelley's *Frankenstein*, and in the twentieth century it was used again by Karel Capek in his play *R.U.R.*, which is about a war of robots against humans. Two popular movies—*2001* and *Alien*—tell stories about intelligent nonhuman devices that seek to destroy their human companions.

In addition to demonstrating that the motifs of benign and malign nonhuman intelligence life go deep in the human psyche, these precedents remind us that references to the creative and destructive potentials of intelligent machines are by no means new to the twentieth century, and their long hold on the imagination helps to explain why they have caused—and continue to cause—such ambivalent responses.

Let us now turn to the main subject.

One of the key figures in the early development of computers is Alan Turing, who demonstrated in 1937 that digital computers were—in theory—capable of solving any computable problem. In 1950, soon after his theory had been vindicated by the first working digital computers, Turing wrote another remarkable paper titled "Computing Machinery and Intelligence." This paper begins with the announcement, "I propose to consider the question, Can machines think?"

Turing did not argue that machines *could* think; instead, he argued, essentially, that what we need is a test to show they can't. This is called "the Turing Test." I will return to it, but for the moment the important point is that Turing thought machines would eventually be able to pass his test. He wrote, "I believe that at the end of the [twentieth] century, the use of words and general educated opinion will be altered so much that one will be able to speak of machines thinking without expecting to be contradicted."

Instead of being chuckled over by the experts and then dropped into the scientific memory hole, the metaphor of machine life—and especially, machine intelligence—has persisted. Interestingly, it has persisted in scientific literature—sometimes to the irritation of those scientists who consider it misleading and sensational—as well as in popular literature.

In an article on technology in the year 2000 published in MIT's *Technology Review* in 1969, Philip Morrison, a highly regarded professor of engineering at MIT, referred to "Computer-based life, which will have such properties of self-reflection and rapid communication that all of us will be taxed to distinguish them from the thought of man. Turing had this dream, and I think we will not pass the turn of the century before we realize it in some degree." The metaphor was still useful twenty years later to Robert Jastrow of NASA's Goddard Institute, who referred in an article titled "The Thinking Computer" to the abilities manifested by computers as "non-biological intelligence, springing from human stock, and destined to surpass its creator."

Here it will be useful to consider the relation between metaphors of machine life and metaphors of machine evolution.

In a free use of anthropomorphic metaphor, libraries might be described as "artificial memories of civilization." In them knowledge is materialized in a way that is independent of any single human mind. Libraries are, however, inanimate. They have order and coherence, but it would be hard to find any reason to imagine them as living organisms.

Simple mechanical devices created from cogs, levers, springs, and screws have striking internal regularities. They are perhaps like crystals. They exhibit a strong sense of self, and they are capable of endless surprising variations on their simple norms. They can even be made to look and behave like little animals and people, but no one would think of them as living or even as having characteristics that might make anyone think they are living. These are, you might say, metaphors that remain resolutely and irredeemably metaphoric. In fact, their metaphoric quality is often emphasized by their design. Mechanical soldiers and toy animals are intentionally designed as caricatures of real soldiers and real animals—caricature emphasizes their artificiality, hence the fact that they are "likenesses," not "identities."

If simple machines are a little like crystals, a clock with an escapement mechanism might be compared to an elementary protein. It has a complexity that is self-referential and therefore is especially rich with potential. An escapement mechanism is a kind of governor, and it regulates the unwinding of the clock's weights or springs. Its self-regulation involves feedback. In a limited way, it asserts control over its own actions. As Norbert Wiener points out in the preface to his groundbreaking 1948 book *Cybernetics*, the word "governor" has the same root as "cybernetics." It is the Greek word for "steersman," which means that "governor" is, itself, a kind of metaphor of machine life.

The Analytical Engine proposed by Charles Babbage in 1834 went far beyond clocks and governors. It was intended to think. It would think exclusively about numbers—tide tables, for the most part—but it would think about them intelligently enough to say things useful to humans who listened to it.

The plan was brilliant but the machine was a failure. Mechanical devices can add, subtract, multiply, divide, and sort within limits, but the limits are fairly narrow. When they become complicated, they encounter the liabilities of all mechanical systems: inertia, friction, inaccurate machining, slippage, distortion, fatigue, breakage. Nevertheless, mechanical calculating machines can perform limited tasks quite efficiently, and they became common well before the First World War. Devices to input and record information were also developed. Babbage had used a system of cards based on the cards used by Joseph Jacquard to control weaving patterns for mechanical looms. A variation on this system became the basis for a highly profitable line of statistical and calculating devices developed by Herman Hollerith, an American, for his Tabulating Machine Company, which later changed its name to International Business Machines.

During the Second World War, under the pressure of such urgent tasks as deciphering codes and tracking high-altitude aircraft with gun batteries, calculating machines were radically improved. The men responsible for their improvement avoided the limitations that defeated Babbage by using electrical circuits rather than physical devices like cogs and levers and wheels.

The first modern computers emerged between 1944 and 1950. They were huge and ungainly, and in spite of the apparent complexity of their spaghetti-like circuitry and glowing tubes, they were more like viruses or perhaps the earliest protozoa of carbon-based evolution than advanced organisms. By 1960 they had progressed from vacuum tubes, through transistors, to silicon chips. They had slimmed down, and although their circuitry consistently grew more complex, they lost their clumsy appearance. They looked increasingly elegant as they swam through the ocean of possibility out of which they had emerged.

By 1975 integrated circuits and co-processing had arrived. These developments made possible computing systems that might, in an extension of the evolutionary metaphor, be compared to primitive multicelled organisms. We are not talking here about multicelled creatures organized into complex systems and subsystems, but of simple systems that are closer to cooperative cell colonies. Nevertheless, even this kind of progress represents a decisive step upward on the evolutionary ladder. It took perhaps a billion years for carbon-based life to progress from single-celled to multicelled creatures. Silicon devices made a comparable advance in twenty-five years.

The advance is apparently continuing. In August, 1988, the Department of Defense proposed a $400 million research and development program for machines using neural networks. Note that the metaphor of machine life is explicit in the term "neural network." A machine using a neural network is intentionally designed to be "like" a carbon-frame system of neurons—that is, a brain. In fact, the "likeness" cuts both ways. Designers of neural networks have been influenced from the beginning by studies of the architecture of the brain—most especially by studies of the visual system that extends from the retina of the eye to the visual cortex of the brain. By the same token there has been great interest among neurologists in so-called "reverse-engineering," which uses lessons learned from the design of neural networks to create and test models of neuron function. Evidently, machines *are* becoming more lifelike, and as this is happening, it is becoming possible—and useful—to use them as models-admittedly crude-for understanding the brain. However, for all of their advances, machines are still in their evolutionary infancy.

Craig J. Fields, Deputy Director of the Defense Advanced Research Projects Agency (DARPA), is one of the strongest advocates of neural networks. Fields wants to fund a new generation of neural computers that will approach bees in intelligence. A bee, one might say, is not very intelligent, but it is a lot more intelligent than an association of cells. In an interview, Fields observed, "Bees are pretty smart.... Bees can evade. Bees can choose routes and targets." (It becomes clear from these remarks why Fields and the Department of Defense are interested in bees—and neural networks; but if they weren't, somebody else would be.) Whatever the I.Q. of bees, it took some three hundred million years after the appearance of multi-celled organisms for carbon-based evolution to produce them. If Fields is right about neural networks, it will take silicon devices about fifteen years.

It may be added that the metaphorics of machine evolution includes the ills as well as the desirable aspects of carbon life. In the summer of 1988, between six thousand and fifty thousand computers (depending on which newspaper one reads) were crippled by a small, self-replicating program called a "virus." Other computers have been attacked by parasite-like creatures called "worms."

*   *   *

So much for the intelligence of bees. What about the human sort of intelligence? Here numerous qualifications are necessary. As has just been pointed out, no machine, considered as an entity, has approached even the bee in intelligence, if intelligence is considered as a measure of the ability of the creature to adapt in real time to rapidly changing conditions in the environment. On the other hand, if intelligence can be segmented into the abilities needed for different kinds of tasks, it is obvious that in some respects computers are very smart indeed. If Babbage had been able to build it, the Analytical Engine would have far surpassed humans at calculating—known more familiarly as "number-crunching." The first-generation computers created during World War II were much faster and far more versatile than the Analytical Engine could ever have been, and they worked.

On the other hand, number-crunching and equation solving—even when the equations are complex—seem narrow skills in comparison to the skills in human intelligence. Humans use logic more often than mathematics. Can computers perform the sorts of analysis that require logic? Chess is a supremely logical game, and it is usually considered a game that requires a great deal of intelligence to play well. Can computers ever play chess? And there are still more general skills than logic, skills that require the mysterious and very human talent called "common sense" and that can deal with the endless imperfect and "fuzzy" situations encountered in the real world. Can computers have common sense? Can they deal with fuzzy problems like recognizing a friend's face in a crowd, or understanding words pronounced in different ways?

The question of whether machines can reason logically led in the summer of 1956 to a famous conference at Dartmouth on what researchers were beginning to call "Artificial Intelligence." Two members of the conference—Herbert Simon and Allen Newell—brought a remarkable program to show off. They called it "Logic Theorist" (note the emphasis on logic rather than "fuzzy" situations), and it was able to prove theorems from Russell and Whitehead's *Principia Mathematica*. In other words, it showed that machines could learn to reason as well as to calculate.

By the early 1970s Stanford's Douglas Lenat had created a program called "The Automated Mathematician" that was a significant advance beyond "Logic Theorist." Not only did the new program reason logically, but it seemed to operate independently of human direction by drawing on built-in general rules of procedure called heuristics. It explored set theory, then proceeded to invent arithmetic, and finally, carried out an analysis of prime numbers. Another program developed by Lenat, EURISTIKA, improved on the Automated Mathematician by being able to change its heuristics in the light of experience. By 1982 EURISTIKA had been barred from international competition in the war game "TRAVELLER" because after its second victory, the sponsors of the game decided no human opponent could beat it. This is an interesting development, but it hardly comes as a surprise in view of the superiority of machines, including primitive calculating machines, over humans in the area of number-crunching. What is most interesting about the progress objectified in Lenat's programs is the movement toward self-sufficiency and perhaps even a primitive kind of inner direction. These qualities have less to do with intelligence, I think, than with a sort of "sense of self" that is associated with consciousness. No one would argue that Lenat's programs were conscious—obviously, they had not a scintilla of consciousness—but they surely had qualities that are involved in the phenomenon of consciousness.

During the 1950s the question of whether computers could learn to play a decent game of chess became a kind of litmus test for machine intelligence. It is obviously a corollary of the view of intelligent behavior that led Lenat to call his first program "The Automated Mathematician"—it was doubtless encouraged by association of chess with the life intellectual and the fact that many scientists drawn into the debate about machine intelligence were avid chess players who took considerable pride in their game. The first rudimentary chess-playing programs appeared in the 1950s. They were no match for even moderately accomplished amateurs, but by 1970 machines were offering human players respectable, if not inspired, competition. In a much publicized episode, a prominent philosophical critic of the idea of machine intelligence who had apparently (accounts of the affair differ) scoffed at the idea of a machine being able to play respectable chess was defeated by a machine, much to the delight of the Artificial Intelligence community. By 1980 machines were to play adequate B-level chess, and computer research was turning to more challenging problems like speech synthesis and vision. More recently still, G. Kasparov, a Grand Master, was challenged by a program named "Deep Thought" (note the metaphor of life-even of consciousness). He managed to defeat the program, but only after two hours of play. More and better programs will undoubtedly appear and one is sure eventually to defeat a Grand Master, but the chess problem has already been sufficiently solved to have lost its interest among researchers at the cutting edge of the subject.

Was Turing right? Is it becoming possible—to use his words— "to speak of machines thinking without expecting to be contradicted"?

Hubert Dreyfus, a philosopher at Berkeley, California, who became interested in Artificial Intelligence, felt so concerned about the spread of this sort of speculation that he attacked it in a book published in 1972 titled *What Computers Can't Do*. The book is thoughtful and philosophically sophisticated, but it does not seem to have persuaded anybody who was not already convinced. NASA's Robert Jastrow could still assert confidently in 1982 that "portable, quasi human brains, made of silicon or gallium arsenide, will [soon] be commonplace. They will be an intelligent race, working partners with the human race."

During the 1970s and 1980s there were several other important contributions to the debate. The Turing Test, to which I referred at the beginning of this essay, requires a human operator in communication with a "something" in another room. If, after a suitable period of time, the operator cannot decide correctly whether the "something" is a machine or another human better than half the time, then the test has been passed: the machine cannot be distinguished from a human in a way that improves on pure guesswork.

In a much discussed 1984 lecture titled "Minds and Brains without Programs," another Berkeley philosopher, John Searle, argued that even if a machine passed the Turing Test, it would not be intelligent, because, essentially, it follows rules without understanding what it is doing or why; and in a 1987 book titled *Understanding Computers and Cognition*, Terry Winograd and Fernando Flores, both prominent theorists of Artificial Intelligence, made a similar case. They argued that computers have an inherent "blindness" (a term borrowed from Heidegger) that prevents them from being receptive to the broad range of

cultural inputs that always frames human consciousness and that constitutes the "space of commitments" that gives specific meaning to the
statements (or "speech acts") that an individual makes. If this is the
case, computers obviously cannot be "intelligent" in the sense in
which Winograd and Flores use that term.

I think that Winograd and Flores (and Searle as well) unques-
tionably make a valid point, but I do not think it is exactly the point
that needs making. The issue is not what computers "are" in some
Platonic sense, but how they are incorporated into the closely woven
web of human culture. In a sense, this position is an alternative extension of Heidegger's ideas, concentrating not on the internal status of
machines but on the influence of machines on the "space of commitments" to which Flores and Winograd refer, which is demonstrably
altered by the arrival of those machines and which, in turn, becomes
the force that shapes the consciousness of those born into it. At the
beginning of this essay I called attention to the fact that the boundary
between what is metaphoric and what is direct statement is culturally
determined, and that a large part of this determination is made by the
language that people assimilate in childhood. Computers may seem
"blind" (but note, even here, the metaphor of machine life, although it
is an impaired kind of life) to one generation, but to the next generation the question of whether or not they are "blind" may be irrelevant.
To that generation, in fact, it may seem odd that such a question ever
seemed worth debating.

Let us consider the Winograd-Flores position from a slightly different angle. In one sense Winograd is absolutely right. Computers
are not "intelligent" (or "conscious" or whatever term fits the argument here). He knows this even though machines can seem uncannily
lifelike at times, but he knows this because he knows machines from
the inside. He might be compared to a magician who does not believe
in rabbits in hats because he has been pulling the rabbits out of his
coat-sleeves. On the other hand, the audience in the theater sees only
the trick, and to that audience, the rabbits are demonstrably emerging
from the hat in amazing and delightful profusion. The difference
between a theater and a society is that in society the audience rather
than the performer ultimately decides how reality fits together and
what words mean—including what words are to be understood literally and and what are to be understood as metaphors. As Heidegger,
himself, recognizes, we are creatures of culture, and the term "space
of commitments" is both in some sense a synonym for the culture in
which we live (or that part of the culture that affects us most deeply)
and an explanation of the understanding (including our own understanding) of what we mean when we make statements. To return to

the magician and the rabbits, ultimately, society determines what the magician himself (or his next-generation descendant) believes. Put the matter another way. If we knew as clearly what goes on inside the human brain as Winograd knows what goes on inside of a computer, might we not be tempted to see the operation of the brain as "mechanical"—or, alternately, to regard the whole question of whether it is or is not mechanical as anachronistic?

That is why Turing's original posing of the problem of thinking machines was so brilliant. In his 1950 article he did not claim that we know what thinking is—the implication of his statement is that we do *not* know what it is and maybe never will in any absolute sense. Instead, he argued in practical terms about what we perceive and how we formulate our perceptions in language. Recall the phrasing of his prediction: "I believe that at the end of the century *the use of words and general educated opinion will have altered so much* that we will be able to speak of machines thinking without expecting to be contradicted." Winograd is talking about absolutes—which probably do not exist unless you can see the world from the point of view of God. Conversely, Turing is talking about cultural conditions—in this case, the meanings of words—which most certainly do exist and which form the continuum into which we are born, and about conditions that shape consciousness which are capable of objective description and analysis.

Turing's point is illustrated by the remarkable success of an early program that carried on a dialogue with its user. The program is called ELIZA—note the human name—and is based on nondirective (or Rogerian) therapy. ELIZA was written mainly by Joseph Weizenbaum in the 1960s. Even those users who knew how ELIZA worked were charmed and fascinated by the conversations she carried on, and less knowledgeable users were sufficiently persuaded of her humanity to confide intimate details of their emotional lives to her. The response to the program was so disturbing, in fact, that Weizenbaum says he "came to regret ever having written it."

Disturbing or not, the response of users to ELIZA is hardly surprising. People who are entirely rational and would be shocked to be called superstitious feel affection for tools, guns, an old sweater, the family car. Boats are always given names (usually female), and Henry Ford's Model T was universally known as "Tin Lizzie." It is much easier to feel kinship with something like ELIZA that speaks your language and seems to have your interests at heart than an ocean liner named "Queen Elizabeth" or a car named "Lizzie." And why, after all, should such feelings of kinship be suspect? Charles Lecht, founder of Lecht Sciences, Inc., asks, "Would it make any difference

in our lives if we conceded the idea that machines have an intellect? I
have decided that nothing but good can come of it."

*   *   *

Winograd quotes Daniel Dennett, a philosopher of cognition, to
the effect that "on occasion, a purely physical system can be so complex, and yet so organized, that we find it convenient, explanatory, and
pragmatically necessary for prediction, to treat it as if it has beliefs and
desires and was rational." Dennett calls his position "the intentional
stance." It is useful because it recognizes that machine intelligence is
partly a metaphor—a matter of "as if"—and partly a statement whose
ultimate meaning is determined by intention.

In a society in which there is a regular, easy, and deep inter-
course between humans and devices that converse in natural languages, machine intelligence will be a *de facto* reality regardless of
the logicians. Winograd and Flores assert, "A computer...can never
enter as a participant into the domain of human discourse." That is
probably true for human discourse as it has traditionally existed, but
traditional discourse is not entirely relevant here. "Human discourse"
is plastic. It changes as culture changes. I suggest that the computer
has already entered as a participant into the domain of human discourse, and that it has already revolutionized our view of ourselves
and our world. I do not mean that we stand around talking to robots
(although we listen to synthesized speech almost every time we call
"Information"), but rather, that modern developments in every sphere
of science from biology to medicine to space exploration to plate tec-
tonics to environmental and population studies to metallurgy and far
beyond would be unthinkable without computers and that what we
have learned from our discourse with computers in these and like
fields has *already* profoundly reshaped twentieth-century culture,
quite aside from what may come in the future. As the discourse continues to deepen and ramify, it will change the meaning of the words
that make up the discourse. Winograd and Flores, themselves, make
the point, although I think they fail to give it sufficient weight: "We
exist within a discourse, which both prefigures and is constituted by
our utterances." Isn't this exactly what Turing was saying? Except
that what Winograd calls "existing within a discourse" Turing describes as "the use of words and general educated opinion."

Consider what is already true of our discourse. From the beginning, computers have been referred to in anthropomorphic metaphors
by laymen and scientists alike. From the beginning the public called
computers "electronic brains." Allegedly more thoughtful scientists

agreed that computers speak a "language," have "memories," and use "logic." A computer "reasons" and "understands" FORTRAN or LISP and "plays" chess or checkers or poker. If it can synthesize speech, it is said to "talk." Computers that deal with real-world situations have "sensory input." Their senses can include "vision," "hearing," and "touch." The self-regulation of computers is that of a "steersman"; if they lack certain abilities, they are "blind." Robots "walk" and have "arms" and "fingers" and "see" and "handle" objects. The title chosen by Pamela McCorduck for her excellent 1979 book on the development of Artificial Intelligence is *Machines Who Think*. As I have already noted, computers are also vulnerable to attack by "viruses" and "worms," not to mention "Trojan Horses" and "bombs."

The point can be carried further: is not a major influence on the development of silicon devices the imperative *to make the metaphor of machine life a reality*? That sounds a little odd, but it is the best available explanation for several current representations of machines in relation to humans. Perhaps it can be understood as a modern-dress manifestation of the archetypal feeling that man shares the earth with invisible others who play vital roles in determining his destiny. From earliest times, men have felt a compulsion to make these invisible companions visible. That, for example, is the reason for masks and statues of gods and demons and spirits, including statues in polychrome with realistically contoured robes and inlaid eyes, and, in the case of Christian statues, thorns that bite into the head and blood that trickles in a red stream from the spear-lanced side. Is it not a lighthearted variation on the urge to make the invisible visible that has led from earliest times to the creation of toys in the shape of humans and animals and to the attempt to mechanize these toys—to give them a kind of life—by putting them on wheels, giving them moveable limbs, adding wind-up or spring-driven motors, and by giving animals voices that say "Moo" and "Bow wow" and dolls the ability to cry "Mama" and wet their pants?

This same urge to make metaphors real is an underlying motive of science fiction, where the still-impossible is presented as having been achieved. The robot R2D2 in *Star Wars* is a benign vision of possible silicon intelligence, the machine equivalent of a lovable mascot. But perhaps when the metaphor becomes a reality, the results will be less happy. I have noted that the invisible powers that seem to surround primitive man can be daemonic as well as kindly. Two nightmares that hover just below the surface of the vision of machine life are also objectified in science fiction.

First, machine life may turn out to be malevolent. Fear about this underlies the earliest European drama about robotic civilization, Karl

Capek's *R.U.R.* (1921), where the robots rise up and seek to destroy their human creators and masters. Fear about the malevolence of machine life merges with a second concern—fear that robots may become indistinguishable from people. Capek's robots are androids; that is, they look like people. A similar sinister image of androids is presented in the film *Alien*, in which it is revealed at the climactic moment that the evil force destroying a space mission is a robot that looks like a human and that the other crew members have taken as one of their own kind. Many years ago Norbert Wiener pointed out that it makes no real difference whether a signal comes from a machine or from a human agent. Films like *Alien* suggest that the public is already apprehensive that he may be right, and that one day, humanity may find itself enmeshed in signals that seem human but are, in fact, from machines. Absurd? How many pieces of mail—some dripping with alluring promises and some vaguely menacing—does one already receive daily that are produced by computer rather than a human author? How many of the voices we now hear on the telephone giving the time or the weather or a desired phone number are computer simulations?

The blurring of the distinction between computers and animate beings is being complemented in modern culture by a weakening of the human sense of what reality is. This weakening is the direct result of technology. Movies and television create the illusion of being present at the unfolding of events. Arcade games also create this illusion, and strenuous efforts are put forth to make the illusion especially vivid in a variety of practical training programs—for example, in instrument flying, in the operation of complex weapons like tanks, in law enforcement, in emergency medical procedures, and in architecture and fashion design. A term has been devised for serious efforts to simulate the real so completely that it is indistinguishable from the manufactured: *artificial reality*. At their best, the creators of artificial realities come close to obliterating the difference between world and illusion. The effects they produce are related to other kinds of reality-simulation—for example, to image manipulation in advertising and politics and to the curious but well-documented fact that for many people an event is not authenticated—not "real"—unless it has been captured in a photograph or on television.

Neural networks give added depth to the metaphor of machine intelligence. Such networks seem to have the ability to teach themselves, and in certain configurations, they are, in a sense, programmed by experience, so that the connections they establish as a result of experience become crude—very crude—models of aspects of the world they have experienced. Perhaps one could say that the resulting circuits are analogies—maybe even metaphors—for the world that created them. That sounds moderately human, and those who design them usually prefer to speak of their machines as "learning" skills or being "taught" rather than of "programming" them. A measure of the androidal quality of discussions of neural networks is provided by NETtalk created by Terrence Sejnowski while at Johns Hopkins University and Charles Rosenberg of Princeton. The program used a mere 231 "neurons," yet it managed to be self-organizing. Once it had been supplied with phonetic samples of the speech it was to emulate, it taught itself to talk. An article in a 1987 issue of *High Technology* describes the learning process with a veritable cascade of life metaphors: "Like a child, the network starts out untrained, and produces a stream of meaningless babble....The continuous stream of babble first gives way to bursts of sound, as the network 'discovers' the space between words....After being left to run overnight... NETtalk is talking sense."

Such developments suggest that in the dizzily rapid progress of their evolution, silicon devices have already passed the point at which they are easily distinguishable from carbon-based intelligences. The metaphors assigning them human attributes begin to seem to be less metaphorical and more like statements of fact. In any event, they are more than playful conveniences. They express something about the relation of apparently intelligent machines to contemporary culture in general. That does not mean the machines are alive; it merely means that the culture has adapted to them sufficiently—and vice versa—so that the question of whether or not they are seems less urgent than it did even a decade ago. What is the new relation that is emerging between man and machines? In view of the fact that it is a very new relation, having existed for only forty years or so, what does it imply about the future?

William McLaughlin of the Caltech Jet Propulsion Laboratory attempts to answer that question in a provocative 1983 article in *Interdisciplinary Science Reviews*. Drawing on the metaphor of machine evolution, he argues that computers are developing so rapidly that the days of human supremacy on the planet may be numbered: "Judging that the current direction in machine design is not a dead end...the close of the twenty-first century should bring the end of human dominance on earth." Note that McLaughlin's suggestion about the end of human dominance does not imply the disappearance of man as an organism, only as an idea. The presence of higher organisms on the evolutionary chain has never implied the destruction of lower organisms, as witness the flourishing of protozoa, horseshoe crabs, butterflies, and golden retrievers on the same planet as man. For centuries, however, man has understood himself in terms of the *idea* of his supremacy over the visible universe. The idea is clearly present in Genesis, when Jehovah gives man control over all of the creatures. It is explicit in the literature of humanism and reaches a crescendo in the art and literature of the Renaissance. It is still at the center of Darwin's view of evolution, which, in spite of its much maligned materialism, explicitly regards man as the pinnacle and ultimate justification of the massive and age-old process of natural selection.

*   *   *

When clocks became widespread, they were a great convenience and also—because they allowed precise measurement of time—a great source of discovery about natural processes. They also had an effect, though a less obvious one, on human culture. By making it possible to segment the day precisely, they allowed the establishment of regular work schedules and of standardized hourly wage schedules. As man adjusted to these new conditions, he became more regular in his habits—in other words, more clock-like. The same thing is happening in contemporary culture. In one way or another the changes being created by the new symbiosis between man and machine are leading to a radical revision of the understanding of humanity. It is in this sense, I suggest, that we are presently witnessing a kind of disappearance of man.

The term "disappearance" is evidently another metaphor. Is it merely a matter of new meanings for old words—the changes in language that Alan Turing predicted—or does it go deeper?

If one looks at the relevant literature, several scenarios are evident.

One scenario might be called the steady-state scenario. In this scenario, carbon man will continue to breed, as all other animals continue to breed, in utter indifference to his changed position on the evolutionary scale. Perhaps earth will come to be a kind of galactic game preserve in which rare species, of which carbon man is one, are protected as elephants are now protected in Kenya. Perhaps it is *already* a game preserve. This idea has been seriously proposed by scientists looking for intelligent life elsewhere in the universe. It is called "the zoo hypothesis," and it is invoked to explain the odd fact that no signs of life have been detected, even though common sense and elementary statistics suggest that there is lots of intelligent life in every direction. Perhaps the intelligent life beyond the earth does not want to be observed. Perhaps this life has recognized, as humans seem to have done only dimly, that the presence of a higher species in a closely bounded environment can be terribly destructive to lower species. Perhaps earth has been cordoned off for protection of its carbon-frame species.

Another scenario is sketched by Hans Moravec, senior research scientist at Carnegie-Mellon University's Mobile Robot Laboratory, in his new book, *Mind Children* (1988). "What happens," he asks, "when ever-cheaper machines can replace humans in any situation? Indeed, what will I do when a computer can write this book, or do my research better than I?"

Moravec's answer is that over the long run, man cannot compete directly with machines. Since he cannot beat them, he will have to join with them—or, in Moravec's striking metaphor, he will have to be incorporated with them. Moravec uses the metaphor of transplant surgery to suggest that man may eventually become a cyborg-that is, he may combine some of his spiritual elements with the spiritual and physical elements of machines. This is already happening through increasingly varied use of electrical implants and "smart" prosthetic devices. A not very radical extrapolation from these strategies underlies several popular science-fiction stories, including the recent movie *Robocop* and the TV series *Max Headroom*.

Moravec describes a mind transplant:

> You've just been wheeled into the operating room. A robot brain surgeon is in attendance. By your side is a computer waiting to become a human equivalent, lacking only a program to run. Your skull, but not your brain, is anesthetized....Though you have not lost consciousness, or even your train of thought, your mind has been removed from the brain and transferred to a machine. In a final, disorienting step the surgeon lifts out his hand. Your suddenly abandoned body goes into spasms and dies.... Your perspective has shifted. The computer simulation has been reconnected to a shiny new body of the style, color, and material of your choice. Your metamorphosis is complete.

Another possibility is suggested in different ways by Edward Fredkin of MIT and William McLaughlin of Caltech. Perhaps the machines will not be a permanent problem because they will disappear.

Near the end of her book, *Machines Who Think*, Pamela McCorduck asks Fredkin whether the intelligent machines of the future will be friends of man. He replies:

> I suspect there will be very little communication between machines and humans, because unless the machines condescend to talk about something that interests us, we'll have no communication. For example, when we train the chimpanzee to use sign language so that he can speak, we discover that he's interested in talking about bananas and food and being tickled and so on. But if you want to talk to him about global disarmament, the chimp isn't interested and there's no way you can get him interested. Well, we'll stand in the same relationship to a super artificial intelligence. They won't have much effect on us because we won't be able to talk to each other.

The computer imagined by Fredkin has already all but disappeared. It has advanced so far beyond the limits of human intelligence that it has very little to say to its human creators, and it has therefore ceased to communicate. For its human companions it is no longer an intelligent machine—it is simply a black box.

What Fredkin suggests through the metaphor of silence is expressed more vividly by Caltech's William McLaughlin as a process of becoming invisible through evolution. McLaughlin's position takes us back to the problem of extraterrestrial life. Why, he asks, have we so far failed to locate any evidence that such life exists? Perhaps it is because this life is so far beyond man on the evolutionary scale that it is invisible to human reason. McLaughlin uses an analogy: "Four thousand million humans share the continents with 10^{15} ants, but not one is aware of our existence as 'advanced ants.'" McLaughlin then extends the analogy to intelligent machines: "We are separated from the ants by some one hundred million years of evolutionary history. With the rapidity of technological evolution, it is reasonable to expect that [computing] machines and their descendants only a few thousand years from now might be invisible."

Of course, the developing symbiosis between man and machine may be entirely benign and free of surprises. The machines may have no effect at all on human culture; or the effect may be so gradual and so supportive of human values that it goes unnoticed, as, for example, a warming trend that continued very gradually over several centuries might not be noticed as long as it did not cause any catastrophic changes like widespread droughts or a sudden melting of the polar ice cap.

There is another possibility. It was explored by A. E. Van Vogt in a science fiction story titled *The Human Operators*. I owe my familiarity with the story to a reference by Christopher Evans in *The*

Micro Millennium (1979). In Van Vogt's story, intelligent space ships have been sent from the earth to explore the galaxy. Each ship carried a human crew to maintain it. The ships eventually escape human control and go off on their own. They continue to meet, however, at regular intervals so that the humans can mate. The humans, meanwhile, have forgotten their past. They have become the passive creatures of the spaceships. There is an interesting evolutionary parallel to this. It is the migration of mitocondria into some Precambrian cell. Once in the cell, the mitocondria were captured, and they have lived there in comfortable and oblivious symbiosis ever since.

*   *   *

Van Vogt's scenario is fanciful. It makes good fiction, but it has no basis in anything that presently looks like fact. For that reason it can be considered a metaphor—and a very poetic one at that—rather than a a rigorous attempt at projection.

But that is the point. For the subject at hand, metaphors have often turned out to be more useful—even more prophetic—than "reasonable projections." In discussing metaphors of machine life, we have seen that within the short span of forty years since the first practical digital computers, what began as wildly improbable metaphors have in some cases become simple realities and in others, metaphors that are now so thin they seem on the verge of losing their figurative status. Meanwhile, ideas so odd that they were not even entertained as metaphors now have status at least as figures of speech and speculative fictions.

Does this not prove that Turing's prediction was right not only in its specifics but also—and much more importantly—in what it implies about the relation between machines and human culture? Recall his words: "I believe that by the end of the [twentieth] century, the use of words and general educated opinion will be altered so much that one will be able to speak of machines thinking without fear of being contradicted."

Machines that think are very new. They are evolving rapidly, and there is no reason to believe, at least for the moment, that their evolution is about to slow down. Much that is important to carbon man—his analytical ability, his ability to calculate, his ability to make fine discriminations—has already been modeled in silicon, and in some areas the model already far surpasses the prototype. A great deal that is still more important to the spirit of carbon man—his soaring imagination, his brilliance, his capacity for vision—may well be modeled in silicon before very long, at least as time is measured in biological evolution. Many undesirable, self-defeating traits will also be filtered out.

If this implies a kind of disappearance, it is one that sounds less like a death than the birth of a higher kind of humanity. William Butler Yeats was thinking of the mechanical devices described by Hero of Alexandria in the fourth century A. D. when he wrote about mechanical birds that sit on golden boughs to entertain "lords and ladies of Byzantium" in his great prophetic poem "Sailing to Byzantium." Whether intentionally or not, the poem's prayer,

> Consume my heart away; sick with desire
> And fastened to a dying animal....,

expresses a yearning for the same kind of transcendence of the purely natural that is often the unspoken point of metaphors of machine intelligence and descriptions of possible future relations between man and the intelligent machines he is creating.

REFERENCES

Blakemore, Colin, and Susan Greenfield, eds. *Mindwaves: Thoughts on Intelligence, Identity and Consciousness* (Oxford: Basil Blackwell, 1987). [Essays by John Searle, Richard Gregory, Philip Johnson-Laird, Roger Penrose, Colin McGinn, Sir John Eccles, Larry Weiskrantz, János Szentágothai,Rodolfo Llinás, Horace Barlow, Nicholas Humphrey, John Crook, Ted Honderich, and others]

Brumbaugh, Robert S. *Ancient Greek Gadgets and Machines* (New York: Thomas Y. Crowell Company, 1966).

Dreyfus, Hubert L. *What Computers Can't Do: A Critique of Artificial Reason* (New York: Harper and Row, 1972).

Evans, Christopher. *The Micro Milennium* (New York: Viking Press, 1979).

Feldman, Jerome A. "Connections: Massive Parallelism in Natural and Artificial Intelligence," *Byte Magazine* (April 1985), 277-84.

Fjermedal, Grant. *The Tomorrow Makers: A Brave New World of Living Brain Machines* (New York: Macmillan Publishing Company, 1986).

Ginestier, Paul. *The Poet and the Machine*, tr. Martin Friedman (Chapel Hill: Univ. of North Carolina Press, 1961).

Hillis, W. Daniel. "The Connection Machine," *Scientific American* 256 (June 1987), 108-15.

Hinton, Geoffrey. "Learning in Parallel Networks," *Byte Magazine* (April 1985), 265-73.

Jastrow, Robert. "The Thinking Computer," *Science Digest* (June 1982), 54-55, 106-7.

Jaynes, Julian. *The Origin of Consciousness in the Breakdown of the Bicameral Mind* (Boston: Houghton Mifflin Co., 1976).

Kinoshita, June, and Nicholas G. Palevsky. "Computing With Neural Networks," *High Technology* (May 1987), 24-31. (New York: E. P. Dutton, 1977).

McCorduck, Pamela. *Machines Who Think: A Personal Inquiry into the History and Prospects of Artificial Intelligence* (San Francisco: W. H. Freeman and Company, 1979).

McLaughlin, William J. "Human Evolution in the Age of the Intelligent Machine," *Interdisciplinary Science Reviews* 8 (1983), 307-19.

Minsky, Marvin, ed. *Robotics* (Garden City, N.Y.: Anchor Press/Doubleday, 1985). [Essays by Marvin Minsky, T. A. Heppenheimer, Philip Agre, Thomas Bionford, Hans Moravec, Robert Freitas, Joseph Engelberger, Richard Wolkmir, Robert Ayres, and Robert Sheckley]

Minsky, Marvin. *The Society of Mind* (New York: Simon and Schuster, 1986).

Moravec, Hans. *Mind Chidren: The Future of Robot and Human Intelligence* (Cambridge, Mass.: Harvard University Press, 1989).

Morrison, Philip. "Intellectual Prospects for the Year 2000," *Technology Review* (January 1969), 19-23.

Restak, Richard M. *The Brain: The Last Frontier* (New York: Doubleday & Company, Inc., 1979).

Searle, John. "Minds and Brains without Programs," see Blakemore and Greenfield.

Simon, Herbert A., and Allen Newell. "Heuristic Problem Solving: The Next Advance in Operations Research," *Operations Research* 6 (January/February 1958), 1-10.

Stevens, John K. "Reverse Engineering the Brain," *Byte Magazine* (April 1985), 287-99.

Tank, David W., and John H. Hopfield. "Collective Computation in Neuronlike Circuits," *Scientific American* 257 (December 1987), 104-14.

Turing, Alan "Computing Machinery and Intelligence," *Mind* 59 (October 1950), 433-60.

Turing, Alan. "On Computable Numbers, with an Application to the Entscheidungsproblem," *Proceedings of the London Mathematical Society* 2. 42 (1937), 230-65.

Wiener, Norbert. *Cybernetics; or, Control and Communication in the Animal and the Machine* (Cambridge, Mass.: MIT Press, 1948).

Wilson, Richard Guy. *The Machine Age in America, 1918-1941* (New York: Harry N. Abrams, 1986). [A profusely illustrated catalogue and commentary on the symbiosis between machines and culture in the first half of this century.]

Winograd, Terry, and Fernando Flores. *Understanding Computers and Cognition: A New Foundation for Design* (Reading, Mass.: Addison-Wesley Publishing Company, Inc., 1987).

2 : 2

CHAOS AND SCIENTIFIC KNOWLEDGE

James A. Yorke

I've long been a science fiction buff, but there's an annoying aspect of most science fiction—if you read science fiction ten to twenty years old, or older, you'll notice the writer had no idea of how today's computer would differ from what he used at that time. You find computers of the distant future clanking and grinding out square-roots of numbers, using paper tape or computer cards. The writers exhibit no imagination. Today we see the computer on little chips. The central processing units of a desktop computer are capable of doing almost all of the work of the best computers of a dozen years ago. We try to extrapolate to the future of computers, but we cannot. Dr. Hardison has given us a vision of what *might* happen; it seems clear that what *will* happen is very different from what we are experiencing today.

A computer on a little chip can have the equivalent of a million transistors—but that is still many millions of times simpler than a human brain (although it is hard to quantify the number of connections in the human brain). The computer is, however, a million times *faster* than a human brain. As we sit in front of a chessboard sorting out positions, it is fair to say that the best players are considering the most relevant positions and sorting them out at, perhaps, one position a second, while a computer uses a totally different technique. The computer is, in fact, very stupid and very fast. It looks at all the positions that could possibly arise after a couple of moves and tries to decide the merits of the final resultant positions-basically using a brute-force approach.

But the brute-force approach of a computer can do wonderful things—let's imagine twenty or so years from now when, for the price of a new car, you will be able to purchase a computer that is a million times more powerful than any computer on earth today. What will it be able to do? While I can't think in terms of that millionfold increase in power, I am a mathematician and I can ask what difference it will make in the field of mathematics.

The first person to have designed an internally programmed computer, John Von Neumann, was a mathematician. One of his objectives was to produce a computer that could prove theorems. In the past year alone there have been at least five conferences on computers proving theorems—two years ago, there were probably none. Times are changing. The theorems which are now being proved are not everyday, run-of-the-mill theorems. They are very special. They are theorems that can be proved with brute force, repetitively using very simple rules. Thus, one challenge to the intelligence of the mathematician is to try to find problems which can be put into such a simplistic format.

I am also interested in computer-generated pictures; my interest is concentrated on pictures which deal with chaotic motion. *Chaos* is a technical term which describes a view of the world which is very different from that of the clocklike universe, the view accepted by scientists of the eighteenth and nineteenth centuries. *Clocklike* is defined as regular, undeviating, and precise; therefore, predictable, even in the long run. We find, with the use of computers, that the universe is not regular or predictable. We really knew that already. We also know what chaos means. While defined by Webster as a state of things in which chance is supreme, we now understand *chaos* as a situation where you know what is happening now and in the near future, but you can't predict what is going to happen in the longer run. The weather is chaotic. We can predict the weather with excellent success over a short period of time, but we don't know what the weather is going to be like five days from now. That's chaos. As another example, imagine your boss walking into your office and saying, "We need your desk, you're fired." Now, that's chaos! That is what we can now study mathematically, but not for complicated systems, like those we meet in real life, but for simplistic, ideal cases. I'm going to show you some pictures but I won't describe all the features of these images.

Figures 2.1 and 2.2 are maps or charts. Although these pictures are incredibly complicated maps, they only report the action of a pendulum. If you are reading a map, you might imagine that, if you looked at it very closely, you might be able to see all the detail you want. Figure 2.2 is a blowup of a small area of figure 2.1. We could create a series of even more detailed pictures, but the remarkable thing is that each turns out to be just as complicated as the one before. These pictures are the result of huge numbers of computations. We are actually augmenting human vision with an instrument here, an instrument sufficiently complex that it restricts our ability fully to

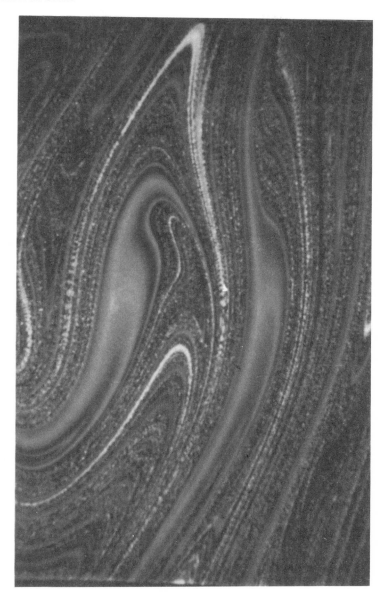

Figure 2.1 Plot describing the movement of a forced, damped pendulum. Angular displacement, Θ, is plotted against angular momentum, $d\Theta/dt$. The dark areas of the figure are either red or blue. Red points correspond to clockwise rotation, blue points correspond to counterclockwise rotation. In the light areas of the figure the direction of motion is not uniquely specified, blue and red points are intimately mixed. Further details are given in *Science* 238 (30 October 1987), 632-37.

Figure 2.2 A small region of figure 2.1 recomputed and magnified, showing, on a finer scale, how points corresponding to clockwise and to counterclockwise motions are inseparable.

understand its output, or to state whether the picture it produces is completely correct.

We mathematicians are frequently asked whether we believe that pictures such as these are correct. This is nothing new. The first person who, for scientific purposes, augmented his vision with an instrument was Galileo, nearly four hundred years ago, and he got into trouble.

If I can paraphrase my idea of the conversation that might have transpired then: Pope Urban VIII said, "Look, Galileo, if you want to overthrow this particular section of church doctrine, fine. Just *prove* that you are right." In fact, the church did not take an absolutist point of view on many of the questions being discussed. However, Galileo said, "Look through this chunk of glass in a tube. Do you see those little dots near Jupiter? Obviously, ..." And, he went on to make various conclusions based on observation. In the meantime, the pope wondered what was actually going on in Galileo's mind—trying to prove his point and overthrow church doctrine just by looking at little dots of light in a glass tube. Today, not many people would take the side of the pope. Is there anyone who would take the side of the pope?

Well, I have an admission to make—I would. You see, I'm a mathematician and mathematicians have certain standards for knowledge, absolute standards, just as Pope Urban VIII did. So I can identify with his problem because, when we see this fuzzy picture coming up on a computer screen (another chunk of glass in a tube), we have to ask ourselves, "Is this picture absolutely correct?"

Today, we mathematicians are in a position where we can attempt to analyze with exact rigor whether our computer pictures are telling us what we think they're telling us. In the case of Galileo and the pope, there was no way for Galileo to prove that he was right with the rigor that the pope required. We hope to be able to establish with absolute precision that these computer pictures are correct.

We have made a series of computer pictures which investigate the pendulum. This is a pendulum which has a little clock to keep it moving, so that it doesn't run down. It keeps on moving and can oscillate in infinitely complicated ways. In fact, it can oscillate irregularly forever. If you pick a point in figure 2.1, the color of the point will tell you what's going to happen. Each one of these points represents a way of starting the pendulum. Choosing a point higher in the picture gives the pendulum a faster initial speed. If you pick a red point, the pendulum will end up spinning clockwise forever. However, if you pick a blue point, it will wind up spinning the opposite way forever. I do not have to be completely precise in describing the physical problem because I am more interested in what the resultant picture looks like.

I want you to understand what happens when we zoom in, in effect looking at parts of the chart with a microscope. To do this we must recompute a small detailed part of the chart. As we zoom in on points which are on the border of a colored region, the picture remains complicated. Conversely, if we were to zoom in on a green point, the screen would be filled with green and, if we zoomed in on a red point, it would be all red. What happens as we zoom in on a boundary point is that the picture remains complicated, no matter how closely we zoom in. If you don't know exactly where you're starting, because of a small error in picking the initial point, or because you are starting near the boundary between colors, then you do not know the color of the point from which you are starting; and, if you don't know the color of the point from which you are starting, you cannot predict how the pendulum will behave in the long run.

We can see very clearly that a large portion of each computer picture is near the boundary between different colors. Because the boundary is so complicated, we zoomed in on a particular area. We could continue making even more detailed pictures (given sufficient computer power), yet the computer picture would remain very, very complicated. The great complexity of the boundary means that predicting what will happen, even for the pendulum, a very simple device, is extremely difficult.

We do not live in the nice, predictable universe that the scientists of a hundred years ago believed in. The computer is revealing to us a universe that is much more complex. The computer itself has not caused the complication. It has only revealed the complexity that's there.

The chaos of our lives is actually very similar to that demonstrated in the computer picture of our pendulum. If we can understand that a simple pendulum can behave chaotically, then we have a better understanding of the chaos in the universe. The solar system appears predictable. However, we are seeing a five-billion-year-old system, one that appears clocklike only because those particular asteroids, comets, and other debris, which were previously chaotic, collided with other bodies and were destroyed. We are actually seeing the remnants of a very dynamic ancient system. Even now, the solar system has chaotic motions that are unpredictable in the long run. Remember, chaos is defined as being predictable in a short run, but unpredictable in a longer run (just like the predictability of your job, or health, or spouse or children; or like the weather).

I view these pictures as a different type of art. But, of course, this is computer art, so perhaps it's not considered "true" art. Nevertheless, these pictures are artistic, like the work of a photographer of mountains, who chooses a view (or two or three) to reveal something that already exists (which he did not create).

Whether or not this work is viewed as art, I see it as showing us a potential that artists have not realized. What we have here is variations on a theme. As you look at the different parts of the picture you see similarities throughout it, even on very small scales, just like the pieces of a musical composition. Perhaps, it is more fitting to liken it to music since, throughout the entire computer picture, you see variations on a single theme, including tiny variations on a small scale, which Western artists have not yet been able to capture.

Now you have had a brief glimpse of what the motion of a pendulum is like. You have here a simplistic scientific toy that mirrors some of the unpredictability of life. Life is more complicated, but similarly chaotic.

DISCUSSION

Farzad Mahootian (Philosophy & Chemistry, Georgetown): Stimulated by Philip Dick's *Do Androids Dream of Electric Sheep?*, I have become interested in the android human relationship. We have *human* metaphors for machines and machine thinking, but we also use *machine* metaphors to describe human behavior and human thinking. Professor Hardison, what are your thoughts about that?

Hardison: Well, you've really got two questions. What do I think of Philip Dick? And, what do I think about the two-way metaphor? I can answer the second question most quickly and easily.

These metaphors first started being used, in depth, in literature related to computing, *before* Alan Turing. An example is the 1948 edition of Norbert Wiener's *Cybernetics*. (That book represented kind of a false start for computer science, but with the development of neural networks, it is now seen as being much closer to the mainstream.) Wiener had a friend who was a neurologist in Mexico. In the preface to *Cybernetics* he describes how he and his friend decided that a neuron was very much like the off-on circuit in a digital piece of machinery; they actually did anatomical studies of neurons, of the electronic stimulation of neurons, and of the off-on firing patterns of neurons. They thought that neurons were connected to each other as wires are soldered together; they didn't know anything about neurotransmitters or synapses. Today, we recognize that neurons are infinitely more complicated than Wiener and his collaborator believed they were, but nonetheless, the analogy between machines and organic life was important to them in their research, and their research was a step in the direction of understanding how the brain functions. It's my understanding—on the basis of a good deal of general reading in current research in neurology and neuroanatomy—that the development of neural-network computation has stimulated a new phase of analysis of brain anatomy, using the *model* of neural networks as the basis of a new approach. Historically speaking, the line of analysis started by Wiener in *Cybernetics* led to analysis of the visual cortex, and of the whole process of vision—and that [sort of interaction] has been a consistent pattern.

The first attempt to create a self-consciously understood neural network was made by a professor at Princeton—it was called a *perceptron*. It was a machine that tried to duplicate the layering of processing of information that apparently occurs in vision. That [attempt to construct a working model] in turn fed back into the analysis of the visual cortex and of the process of vision. By definition, you're groping in these things; you don't know what you're aiming for in a machine and you don't know what you're aiming for in trying to understand the brain—they are both unknown. There is, I think, a very fruitful, circular relation between the two [projects].

I have had a few discussions with Richard Restack, my colleague here at Georgetown and the author of the book, *The Brain*. It is my understanding, both from the conversations and from the book, that what I'm telling you is close to being an accurate description.

On the second question, concerning Philip K. Dick: it's interesting that you should mention him, a fascinating figure in American science fiction. He was paranoid—I believe paranoid-schizophrenic, as a matter of fact. Throughout his life he had endless delusions. His problems were accentuated by the fact that he sold his science fiction stories for $1000 apiece to publications like *Astounding Science Fiction*. When he got to be popular these stories were resold, and a lot of people made vast amounts of money, while poor Mr. Dick was starving to death. He died in 1984. The last of his science fiction novels, which was called *Radio Free Albermuth*, was made into a spectacular opera which was performed at the Paris Opera. It was called *Velis* and the conductor of the orchestra for that opera was Pierre Boulez. I think that Dick is a fascinating writer but I think, to understand his work, probably one needs to come at it in terms of abnormal psychology as much as through science fiction.

Participant: Computer visual art is highly attractive, and often fascinating, but I am glad you mentioned Pierre Boulez. It seems that it is contemporary *musicians* in rock, jazz, and also classical music, who actually are working with electronic machines and producing very exciting music—the musicians are leading the way. Other will catch up with them, I am sure.

Hardison: I agree with you one hundred percent about the fascinating attractiveness of computer art. I would quarrel with Professor Yorke just a little bit when he said that the pictures he showed are like art, but are not art. I thought it was very powerful stuff. Just as people draw an artificial barrier between science and the humanities, they draw artificial barriers between what is art and what is not art. A good deal of twentieth century avant-garde art has been dedicated to smashing those artificial boundaries.

You may recall that one way in which Deschamps attempted to do that was by exhibiting ready-mades, including a urinal, in art-shows and forcing people to look at these things. Joseph Stella was utterly fascinated and dazzled by the Brooklyn Bridge, which is not normally considered a work of art, and yet is a beautiful and spectacular structure. Gustav Eiffel was a maker of iron bridges; he rotated them ninety degrees and created the Eiffel Tower, which disgusted many people in Paris. But Delauney painted something like ninety pictures of the Eiffel Tower and it has become recognized as a great artistic monument. I think that computer visual art is at least as powerful a medium today as [is] computer music. One spectacular computer artist, David Em of the Jet Propulsion Laboratory, recently had a whole book devoted to his art published by Atheneum. James Blin, a computer scientist and expert in graphics, taught Em how to make graphics, but then Em took off and created. Those of you who have seen *Tron* have seen wonderful sequences of computer art—among the best ever created for movie sequences. I don't know why computers don't seem to be very good at handling language, natural language. Computer poetry is not really as interesting—or as gripping and persuasive—as computer music and computer visual art.

3 : 1

BIOLOGICAL AND HUMAN DETERMINANTS
OF THE SURVIVAL OF SPECIES

Edward O. Wilson

This paper will summarize the biological basis of human nature and its origin, point out the genetic affinity that our own species has with other organisms, and then consider creation itself, the diversity of life on earth, and what we are doing to it.

There are twenty-six pairs of human chromosomes, the same number of chromosomes as those of chimpanzees. High-resolution light microscopy shows striking similarities between the chromosomes of these two species, each of which comprises some one hundred thousand genes and about one billion nucleotide pairs. This reflects the conclusion, agreed upon now by a majority of paleontologists and biochemists working in biochemical evolution, that the human and chimp lines (pongoid and anthropoid-ape lines) separated rather recently, probably between five and ten million years ago.

An important generalization, substantiated from the molecular level up to higher lines, is that *life is self-assembling*. In the case of human beings, as in all other species, chromosomes have come into existence, and then all the phenotypes that the genes housed therein have prescribed, through *largely autonomous processes*. Random mutations have occurred (at the level of the genes by nucleotide substitution and alteration in the chromosome structures). Then extremely rigorous natural selection, through uncounted and uncountable numbers of events over millions of years, has swept out an almost unimaginable number of possibilities, to leave us with the highly selected, reduced set of genetic prescriptions that constitute the human species.

It is the view of virtually all biologists today, not reflected upon enough by intellectuals, that this process is autonomous. That is to say, there is no reason to believe that from the very beginning of life on earth some 3.75 billion years ago to the present, immensely diverse, biosphere, anything more than the processes of blind mutation, recombination, and natural selection are needed to explain the origin of life and its evolutionary development, up to and including human life.

Thereupon is pivoted the clear distinction that remains between two competing "metaphysics" (views of how the world works from the top down, what the meaning of human nature is, indeed, what the meaning of humanity is). On the one side is the scientific-humanistic view that biology is self-assembling, that life has produced itself on earth without any particular guidance. On the other side is the traditional religious viewpoint that guidance has occurred, and is obtrusive and directional, in some manner not yet understood on a material basis. It is the *resolution* of those two viewpoints which is crucial if conjunction is ever to be achieved between science on the one side, as it rapidly expands its domain of inquiry into the origin of the human mind and the physical basis of life, and, on the other side religion and religious thought, reflection upon human spirit as distinct from machine metaphors of the material basis of life. This resolution can come about only by sufficient examination of the origin of human nature, not just as a cultural product that is merely an overlay on a biological heritage, but *through the history* of the human genetic origin, which extended over millions of years.

There is every reason to believe that what distinguishes us from utilitarian machines, however sophisticated, is *purposefulness*, intentionality of behavior, goal-orientation. It is entirely possible—indeed it is believed by a wide range of evolutionary biologists, anthropologists, and others—that intentionality can be understood as a product of natural selection. In other words, we are "survival-machines" which have developed an extraordinary cultural superstructure, and all the feelings that define us as human beings are in fact products of biological natural selection. Let me document this very briefly with an examination of how human behavioral development and cultural evolution can be severely constrained by biological history.

Consider, for example, human vision. We see light-intensity as you would if you used a dimmer-switch to take the illumination of a room up and down. We see light-intensity as *a continuum*. Our visual system is built that way. We also have sensitivity to wavelength-change (what we call "color"), but do not see it as continuous. If we were gradually to change the wavelength of light from the outer limit of red down in wavelength to the outer limit of blue-purple, we would not see continuous change; we would see a transit across four relatively unchanging, basic colors. The physiological basis of this is partially understood. It lies in the construction, at the molecular level, of the color cones of the retina. To some extent it also depends on further processing in the neurons leading to the optical cortex, where we assemble our information on color. There is a fair amount known about the genetic basis of this effect. The location of genes, partially at least on the X chromosome, determines which color pigments and receptor membranes we have, and therefore how we see color.

Given that as a paradigm of how the human sensory system is put together, we can turn to an experiment performed some twenty years ago. Munsell diagrams (standard color arrays varying left to right in wavelength and up and down in intensity) were presented to speakers of some twenty different languages that are, from phylogenetic point of view, very far apart from one another, like Zulu, Mandarin, and English. These speakers were asked to point to positions on the array which correspond intuitively to the words used in their particular language to denote color. Those pointings were averaged together, and mean positions were established for each of these languages. What emerged was a clustering. Those clusters of intuitive positioning of color terms, that have evolved mostly independently in different societies, corresponded to the areas of least ambiguity in the transition across the four basic colors. In other words, people evolving color vocabularies tend to stay away from the areas of most rapid sensory change with changing wavelength. They stay away from the area of greatest ambiguity and cluster their vocabulary in areas of least change, the "modal areas."

Papuan highlanders in New Guinea were given synthetic languages that had been invented for this purpose. Some had color names placed on the modal areas of the Munsell array, and others had color names placed in the ambiguous zone. The languages that had the vocabulary in the modal areas were learned much faster and retained much longer. When given a choice, others in the tribe that had a choice between the placement of the two vocabularies picked the one in the modal areas. Here we have an example in a very simple case of how biology constrains, or can constrain, cultural evolution.

Here is another quick example, one that probably has had considerable effect on the evolution of writing, on visual symbolism, and on art. In experiments in Belgium, subjects were shown visual displays of differing complexity or redundancy. Electrical activity in their brains (the "alpha wave") was monitored and the degree of damping of alpha waves measured. This damping is generally recognized as a measure of arousal; it is tightly correlated with behavioral and subjective psychological arousal. The result was that figures of a *moderate* degree of complexity create far more arousal than figures of any other complexity. The degree of arousal went up many fold at a level of complexity roughly equivalent to ten to twenty turns in a standard maze figure. This may well be an innate human response. It probably is not a coincidence that it is about this level of complexity that exists, world-wide, in glyphs, idiographs, colophons, national flags, escutcheons, corporate symbols, grille-work and many forms of abstract representation.

At this point we are on the edge of speculation, admittedly, but it is worth reflecting that perhaps there is something quite distinctive and idiosyncratic in human sensory perception and information processing, whereby the human species has evolved maximum arousal (possibly as an adaptive trait and with a long genetic history) for a *moderate* level of complexity. If we ever do encounter remarkable beings more advanced than ourselves, we may find, assuming that we could communicate with them, that their sensitivity to complexity is quite different from that of humans. I am now making a point as to what constitutes human nature. We take human nature for granted, as fish take the water in which they swim, or as ants accept their underground galleries and chambers. We have very specific and idiosyncratic perceptions and ways of perceiving, thinking, and problem-solving.

Let me go a little further into the area of art, and even religion, and take up a concept that I have labeled *biophillia*. This is the innate predisposition that we have to affiliate with other organisms, and with particular organisms and kinds of organisms in different ways. Our need to have organisms around us and to utilize them in various ways in our thinking is brought about by strong predispositions: for example, our response to snakes. We see in snakes one of the few objects toward which people most readily form true phobias. The most conspicuous others are running water, wolves, spiders, heights, enclosed spaces; all ancient enemies of humankind.

It is very difficult to eradicate fears that cause lower autonomic response, nausea, cold sweats, fast heartbeat, and the like. We know that snakes have, from time immemorial and throughout the world, been an important source of mortality in human beings. Human beings share with other primates worldwide a discernible response to serpent-like motions. Human beings have a quickness to learn aversive behavior to serpent-like forms. In many primates this is accompanied by a specific signal, which appears to be quite peculiar to each species, by which individuals communicate with one another about the presence of a snake. Some species of monkeys in the African tropical forest are even good herpetologists. They can distinguish certain species of snakes as poisonous.

The propensity that human beings have to regard snakes with some fear and to develop deep aversive responses to them is innate, although we can be trained out of it or taught to avoid it. Associated with this is the fact that snakes appear in our dreams more than any other kind of animal. They apparently occur in dreams with nearly the same frequency in dwellers of Manhattan as they do in people who live in equatorial Africa, where there are real snakes that endanger lives. Again and again, such dreams get translated into "the serpent" and similar phantasmagoric forms that are readily read out by shamans and prophets into mythic themes. Thus, we find snakes in consistent roles in art, mythology and religion throughout the world. They play consistently patterned roles in which there is an amalgam of fear, awe, and respect. Humans ascribe to serpents the ability to heal as well as to destroy. Serpent images dominate a great deal of religious art and religious mythology.

Let me give you another example of a possible biophilic response of human beings. Around the world, when given a free choice of where they want to put their dwelling, where they would like to be most of the time, human beings consistently move to an elevated site overlooking park-land, that is, open greensward with scattered trees and copses, and most especially next to a body of water. That's the ideal place to live. That's where the rich and the powerful congregate, characteristically. It's where we build our parliament buildings and our sacred dwellings, and where we tend to find the ideal environment as described in literature and art of peoples all over the world.

It may not be coincidence that such a highly distinctive environment, imitated, for example, in gardens of traditional China and Japan, is very similar to the African savanna environment in which the human species is believed to have evolved. There is a real possibility that there are severe constraints, evolved biological constraints, on the way human beings have generated their cultures, and on the way we will continue to generate our cultures and our value systems, which in turn predetermine what we consider to be beautiful.

Ideal degree of complexity and ideal spatial arrangement may be reflective of millions of years of genetic history to a much greater degree than generally considered in the past. Perhaps, at a deep level, our human culture is even more reflective of genetic history than it is of the particular episodes that constitute modern history, which themselves may represent a hypertrophy, a growth upon basic human tendencies.

With biophillia in mind, let me pass on to a matter of contemporary concern. That is our relation to the remainder of life on earth and what we are doing to it. As a biologist interested in the origin of the human mind, I have seen a strong connection between biological methods, perspective, and ways of viewing human nature and our deep need to be concerned with the remainder of life on earth, as part of the natural environment in which we have evolved and now live. We need to protect the remainder of life for our own physical and mental health.

Recently, with the help of other specialists, I have assembled figures for the diversity of organisms and numbers of species. I don't want to dwell on technical details of natural history, but the present time-period is one dominated, on the land, by two groups of organisms. In diversity and also in biomass, the insects have the overwhelming number of species of organisms in all environments. Their partners for some one hundred and fifty million years, the higher flowering plants, are second. These two groups of organisms own the terrestrial world now, and have done so for the last hundred and fifty million years. Insects, for some reason not fully understood, dominate in terms of diversity at the species level.

I go regularly to the rain forest of Central and South America, primarily to collect ant species (some of the 10^{15} ants that are with us on this earth). Every time I go to collect ants, and every place that I go, I discover new species within hours of entering the field. This is an experience that is common for biologists, other than those who work on the best-known groups such as birds, reptiles, mammals, and plants. Up to the present time scientists have described fewer than two million species of organisms, but it is now believed likely that at least ten million species exist on earth, and more than thirty million species have existed on earth. This is still a poorly explored planet.

Fully one-third of animal biomass is made up by the eusocial insects (highly social insects organized into advanced societies with castes and complicated chemical communication). If we take the insects alone, eusocial insects (ants, termites, wasps, and bees) make up 80% of the entire insect biomass. For one hundred million years the social insects have dominated the terrestrial environment. In the sea, the fringing reefs, where much of the heaviest biomass and greatest species diversity exists, have been dominated by highly social colonial organisms, including corals and sponges.

The most social of all vertebrate species are human beings. We pull the trick off with our learning ability and our imperfectly developed capacity to cooperate and hence overcome our natural mammalian rivalries and aggressions. This one species, in the last few hundred thousands of years, has come to dominate the mammals. The weight of all the humans is now about equal to the weight of all the ants (5×10^9 of us as opposed to the 10^{15} of them). All humanity now weighs approximately as much as all the ants, for the first time in history. We will soon pass them. (I think that's a big mistake.) The social way of life is an exceedingly successful strategy and represents the latest (who can say, perhaps the final) major advance in the evolutionary path that life has followed.

Diversity originates by a process called "adaptive radiation It is displayed in perhaps the most familiar and dramatic form in the adaptive radiation of mammals on the "great" continents: Australia, South America, and the "World Continent." (Africa, Europe, Asia, and North America combined is called "the world continent" by biogeographers, because these land-masses have been close enough together during the past several tens of millions of years to allow reasonably free exchange of organisms across them. South America was an island continent until about three million years ago.)

These three major land masses were sufficiently isolated from one another during the last sixty-five million years of the Cenozoic era for separate mammalian faunas to evolve on these three land masses by the multiplication of species and the filling, into similar niches, of species in genetically very unlike organisms. Thus, in Australia a remarkable marsupial, the Tasmanian wolf, is the ecological equivalent of the big cats, canids, and dog-like mammals of the Old World. In South America, there were completely independently evolved marsupials, now extinct, which closely resembled cats, even down to fine details. There were even marsupials much like the saber-tooth cats that evolved on the world continent as predators on giant mammals.

The most beautiful, and from the point of view of the evolutionary biologist the most striking, of all the adaptive radiations involved the honey-creepers of Hawaii. These birds number twenty-odd species today, and included many more species in the past. They evolved, apparently from a single species, to fill many niches. In Hawaii this was made possible by the isolation of the islands, and the fact that few species were able to migrate from the mainland to Hawaii during several millions of years of evolution. From a single ancestor species, there evolved: finch-like seed-eating forms, warbler-like insect-eating forms, nectar-feeding forms that are similar to hummingbirds, and even a woodpecker-like species, with a chisel-like bill to pick up insects from rotting wood. Some one half of those species were eliminated by the first Polynesian colonists, perhaps two thousand years ago. European settlers have eliminated a number more.

The fate of the earth may be similar to what we now see on the island of St. Helena. This remote South Atlantic island is so far removed from either South America or Africa that it did not acquire ordinary trees, shrubs, and woody species by colonization. As on other remote oceanic islands, the plants that did get there and subsequently evolved into forms like shrubs and trees were "composites", relatives of daisies and sunflowers. Over a period of many hundreds of thousands of years, these produced forests by evolutionary radiation, so that there were tree-daisies and tree-sunflowers. These are superficially indistinguishable from ordinary forest trees, but a close inspection shows that they have an entirely different evolutionary origin. This remarkable forest, this evolutionary laboratory, this wonder of the natural world, once clothed all St. Helena. By the late nineteenth century it had been completely stripped away, leaving the landscape with only a few species remaining.

This is what we are now doing on a worldwide basis. The great majority of species that we know today, especially in the terrestrial environment, live in the tropical moist closed forest (the rain forest). By this time, most of you have heard about the crisis in the rain forest. Three years ago the rapid removal of rain forests was almost unknown to the general public, and even to most biologists, but now we see this as one of the major global environmental problems.

I like to call this the "fourth horseman of the environmental apocalypse." The first three are ozone depletion, the greenhouse effect, and toxic pollution. The fourth is species extinction due to removal of natural habitat, particularly the tropical rain forest. You may remember from the Book of Revelations that the fourth horseman, rider of a pale horse, was death. The other three horsemen were ancillary to the fourth. To call rainforest-depletion "the fourth horseman" is to use an appropriate metaphor.

The tropical rain forest is typically found in an area of two hundred centimeters or more of annual rainfall, allowing broad-leafed evergreen trees to grow in profusion, and in three or more stories. The highest story is typically one hundred to one hundred twenty feet above the forest floor. There is relatively little undergrowth because the light reaching the bottom is limited. The area covered by tropical forests is down about forty-five percent from what it was before humanity began to spread around the world. Today such forests cover about six percent of the land surface of the world. Yet most biologists would agree that they have within them more than half of the species of organisms on earth. These forests are being removed by deforestation and burning at a rate of approximately one percent a year, or one hundred thousand square kilometers (the area of the Netherlands and Switzerland combined) each year, roughly half a football field per second. The effect on species diversity in this great treasure-house of life is catastrophic.

To give you an idea of how much is being removed and how little we know of it, there is a single tree in Peru from which I recovered forty-three species of ants belonging to twenty-six genera, all living on that *one* tree. That is approximately the same amount of diversity, the same number of species, as occurs in all the British Isles. When a forested ridge in Peru was recently clear-cut, ninety species of flowering plant were extinguished in one stroke. These species were probably tens of thousands to millions of years old.

When forests are cut for timber or for agriculture, it is found that over two-thirds of the area of the tropical forest is underlayered by extremely poor soil, which retains nutrients from the forests for only two to three years before becoming sterile semidesert. In one of the sites I know in Brazil you can put one foot in the virgin rain forest with hundreds of species of trees per square kilometer and you can put the other foot in a semidesert, with almost all the biological diversity removed and not likely to return. For this reason, cutting the forest is removal of a nonrenewable resource and causes a tremendous amount of ecological damage, as well as an increase in poverty in many areas.

Studies being conducted by the World Wildlife Fund, Yale Forestry School, and by others, have shown that the forests are rich in species that are potentially productive in latex, in many types of fruit, and in fiber substitutes. If we could develop an extractive economy to utilize this wealth, we would produce more income for the people in the area than would be produced by cutting the forest. This is an important consideration for economic planners, for foreign-aid experts, for politicians in the Third World, and for advisors on foreign policy.

When you remove even one species you are removing a tremendous part of the human heritage without knowing what you are doing. The genetic code of one of the smaller viruses contains about a thousand bits of information. The DNA of the *e. coli* bacterium, used so prominently in molecular genetics, contains approximately one million bits of information in its nucleotide pairs. A typical butterfly, bird, moth, or any of the higher eukaryotic organisms, contains information that is between one million and ten million times the amount of information of the virus. We are extinguishing such species at the rate of more than ten thousand per year by cutting the tropical forest.

To give you another idea of how much information there is in a species, if you were to take the DNA from one cell of a mouse (a typical eukaryotic organism about which we have a good deal of information) and spread the molecule out fully, its four strands would stretch for about one meter, but the molecule would be invisible because it is only twenty angstroms wide. If you were to magnify that molecule until you could see it, let's say until it was as wide as a piece of wrapping string, the molecule would stretch for approximately nine hundred miles. Along each inch of those nine hundred miles, there would be approximately twenty letters of the genetic code.

This information was put together over thousands or millions of years of evolution. We know from those groups where the fossil record is sufficient to make the estimate that the average life-span of a species and its immediate descendants is between one and ten million years. The heritage we are squandering is an ancient one.

The number of scientists who are interested in tropical biology is increasing exponentially now. This is fortunate for the task of saving biodiversity on earth. As a consequence of rapid human growth, coupled with technological advance, and of heedless conversion of natural environments to plant the twenty or so species of food crops that our paleolithic ancestors happened to chance upon in the fertile crescent and in Meso-America, we see a decline in the natural environment and also a decline in arable land.

The highly cooperative way of life of our species has enabled us to spread over the earth and to become the dominant mammalian species. Our thoughtless destruction of natural environments, such as rain forests, is bring about the extinction of many species and puts *our own* survival in serious danger.

DISCUSSION

Participant: Professor Wilson, you have come under criticism from feminist theorists, notably from Dr. Ruth Blier, especially in regard to your book *Sociobiology*. In light of the criticisms you have received, have you reexamined or altered your methodology or your conclusions about social behavior? Do you think that in the evolution of sociobiology as a science, it will ever be compatible with feminist theory? For instance, you mentioned that what constitutes human nature hinges on specific idiosyncratic processes which are the result of natural selection; this comes into conflict with the nature-nurture approach. Feminist theory emphasizes *cultural* influences on human development and on behaviors such as aggression/submission and passivity/domination.

Wilson: I have suggested all along that the old paradigm of full cultural determinism would inevitably have led to drift, [and would have produced] immensely greater diversity and plasticity of human behavior than, in fact, we see demonstrated. I believe that the evidence we have seen in the last few years, [has demonstrated] the genetic prescription of many human behaviors, personality traits and mental states, even getting down to the physiological and neurotransmitter levels. More and more evidence is coming in concerning commonalities of human behavior that appear to have an adaptive basis, suggesting that we are not in the thrall of pure cultural determinism. Purely cultural or historical, non-biological explanations will never be adequate. There is now a whole new school of sociobiology which is developing new theories of biocultural evolution, or gene-culture co-evolution, that I think will help resolve this problem, recognizing clearly that we need to understand *both* the biological basis of history, and *also* cultural history as the *arena* within which a great deal of natural selection, leading to specific genetic propensities, has occurred—as the environment that has imposed upon these prescriptions a very large amount of variability. In other words, [human cultural evolution is] to be treated, I believe, as a very complicated—but in many ways not exceptional—case of gene-environment interaction.

3 : 2

COOPERATION AND INDIVIDUALITY:
IMPLICATIONS FOR
THE FUTURE OF HUMANITY

Louise B. Young

In 1883, Francis Galton made a suggestion which was truly remarkable for his time. He said :

> Our part in the universe, may possibly in some distant way
> be analogous to that of the cells in an organized body, and
> our personalities may be the transient but essential ele-
> ments of an immortal and cosmic mind.[1]

Ideas similar to Galton's are beginning to take shape in some of the philosophical writings of present-day scientists. My thoughts on the role of cooperation and individuality in human societies are based on my own interpretation of cosmic evolution, which places unusual emphasis on the phenomena of convergence, coherence, and increasing complexity.

If we review the history of the cosmos, beginning with the chaotic plasma of matter and energy that erupted from the Big Bang, up to the intricately organized assemblies of matter in the stars and galaxies that we find in the universe today, and on a smaller scale the coherent activity of billions of cells cooperating in living things, we recognize that a form-building process has taken place throughout time, making ever larger, more capable self-organized systems which are built out of separate individual units, thus creating one from two or more. For example, nucleons are built of quarks; atoms are built of nucleons; molecules are built of atoms; cells are built of molecules; organisms are built of cells. Each of these systems is a self-integrated whole. Its form is not imposed from outside, it is maintained from within. It actively retains its own identity, returns to maximum stability after it has been disturbed, and even, to a certain degree, regenerates its form when it has been fractured. These qualities are apparent in living matter and the word "organism" has been used to define them. But units of inorganic matter—like the proton, the atom, the molecule, or the crystal—also possess these characteristics of self-organization as well.

It is notable that the individual units of each level act as the building blocks for the next higher level of complexity and, therefore, at each stage the system is built of larger more complex entities, and each stage opens up a whole new range of potentialities. In general, when units converge to form a larger whole, the integrity of the individual units is not sacrificed. Electrons càn enter and leave an atom as single identical units of matter-energy; when a crystal is melted the molecules that composed it disperse again as separate entities; the sponge can be broken down into many independent living cells; termites retain their own existence even while participating in an elaborately organized society.

I realize that the very mention of termites—or ants or bees—in this connection arouses a fundamental fear in people—the fear that human societies might become like colonies of social insects and modern man doomed to become a specialized worker in a rigid social machine. I will argue that this is an ungrounded fear. There are important differences between the two kinds of society.

The role of genes in controlling behavior is very different in the two cases. Each individual insect is genetically controlled, programmed by instinct to do automatically what is best for the whole colony. The individual human being, on the other hand, has achieved through evolution a very high level of personal freedom. Cooperative behavior is voluntary, and the development of reasoning power is responsible for this important change. Reason can override the imperatives which have been built by genetic inheritance.

The emergence of reasoning power has resulted in other important factors that were not present at any previous stage of the form-building process. For example, mankind has invented efficient modes of transferring information; so people can communicate with each other almost as rapidly as do the cells of a single body. The effective organization of any system depends upon a fast and reliable method of transferring messages among the parts that comprise it. But until recently, communication between individual human beings was slow and unreliable. Now we can speak with only a fraction of a second delay to friends on the other side of the earth and information is relayed by satellites to the most remote corners of the globe. The means are now in hand for forging a coherent system out of individual people dispersed throughout the world.

Ways have also been invented for overcoming the limitations of time—an accomplishment that no other organism has achieved. The ability to store and pass on knowledge has produced a cultural tradition which grows and undergoes adaptation. Stored in libraries around the world, the collective intellectual life of mankind can be tapped by an individual, who may add an additional contribution of knowledge to it. So although the individual passes away, his thoughts may become part of this collective memory which extends back to the dawn of civilization and indefinitely into the future.

Thus cultural evolution has added new potentialities to the transformation process, superseding—although not replacing—the old biological methods, and moving at a much faster pace, because these elements are more easily modified than physical traits passed down by the genes. In the biological method, genetic information is passed unaltered from one generation to another except for an occasional chance mutation and the effort of any individual organism cannot alter it. But through cultural evolution each person has the possibility of playing an active role in the process and influencing the future.

These remarkable new powers are a source of individual pride and pleasure but they also represent the great danger in the human condition. The degree of freedom which has been achieved so rapidly has not yet been sufficiently tempered by the more slowly developing socializing influences. If the delicate balance between liberty and license, between personal initiative and cooperation with others, cannot be established soon, mankind will have failed to meet this extraordinary challenge, because—as we have seen—it is in the convergence, the making of a new coherent system, that the important steps in evolution occur. And now for the first time in the cosmic form-building process, the individual units are free to oppose the cooperative action that could lead to a new state of being whose nature we cannot know but can only guess at.

It has been suggested that the next development in the creative process may be the formation of a global or even a cosmic mind. Lewis Thomas said:

> It seems to me a good guess, hazarded by many people who have thought about it that we may be engaged in the formation of something like a mind for the life of this planet.[2]

Rephrasing this concept in more immediate, practical terms, we can imagine that minds communicating with each other around the world could act as a collective mind with capabilities much greater than those of a single brain functioning alone. The emergence of an international scientific community is perhaps a tentative first step in this direction. But it seems apparent that a truly well-integrated collective mind could only be realized in a peaceful and smoothly functioning society. To set our sights high, let us imagine a model state where the integrity of the individual is maintained but each one contributes to the welfare of the system; so the individual life is richer as a part than as a whole. The goal of a society built on this model may seem impossibly idealistic, but it may be the only realistic scenario for the future of mankind. As Buckminster Fuller once said: "The world is now too dangerous for anything less than Utopia."[3]

REFERENCES

1.   Francis Galton, *Inquiries into Human Faculty and Its Development* (London: Macmillan and Co., 1883).

2.   Lewis Thomas, *The Medusa and the Snail* (New York: Viking Press, 1979), 15.

3.   Buckminster Fuller, cited by Peter Russell in Lewis J. Perelman, *The Global Mind: Beyond the Limits to Growth* (New York: Mason/Charter, 1972), 199.

4 : 1

NEURONS, SCHEMAS, PERSONS, AND SOCIETY

Michael A. Arbib

Emergent Properties and Cooperative Phenomena

Hard tables are made of "insubstantial" atoms, yet we know that inter-actions among atoms provide the web of force that gives the table its strength—the whole seems to be more than the sum of its parts. How-ever, the classic notion that "the whole is more than the sum of its parts" is inadequate, in that it uses a notion of "sum" that, while per-haps appropriate for an inert aggregate, cannot do justice to the *new* patterns that emerge when units interact, even in rather simple ways. The battle that is joined is between those who see emergent properties as transcending the properties of the constituents, no matter how rich their interactions might be, and those who seek to explicate these ap-parently new properties by a new and more subtle analysis of the col-lective impact of such interactions.

The former "transcendent" view of emergent properties is that taken in the work of Samuel Alexander and C. Lloyd Morgan, as summarized by Goudge (1967: 475), who notes that:

> The unpredictability of novel [i.e., emergent] characteristics has been taken to imply that their occurrence is unintelligi-ble, something to be simply accepted with 'natural piety,' as Lloyd Morgan and Alexander have said. ... Some have de-clared that novel characteristics are causally disconnected

from antecedent conditions. ... Others have declared that novel characteristics always attach to organic wholes ... and that the existence of these wholes is either an inexplicable fact or is due to a primordial 'whole-making' agency at work in the cosmos.

By contrast, the theory of cooperative phenomena seeks to exhibit more and more cases in which apparently emergent phenomena are not novel in this sense, showing instead how it is that the interactions among a multitude of units yield properties that are absent when those units are considered in isolation. For example, they study how it is that molecules of H_2O can form ice or water or steam and how changes in temperature can effect phase transitions from one of these forms to another, or how it is that an iron bar can hold its magnetization at one temperature but not at another.

In a ferromagnetic material such as ordinary iron, the individual atoms are little magnets. Local interactions of atoms tend to align their magnetic spin in the same direction; thermal motion tends to "randomize" the spins. If the magnet is not too hot, the local interactions can cooperate so that tracts of the material will have their spins with the same orientation. Such a region of parallel spins is called a *domain*. If we provide a strong enough external magnetic field, it can bias the local interactions to get almost all the spins to align themselves with the field, and then there is *one* domain; the material becomes what we call a magnet. It was a basic discovery by Pierre Curie that there is a critical temperature, called the Curie temperature, such that global magnetization induced by an external magnetic field will be retained if the material is below this temperature, whereas thermal fluctuations will dominate local interactions to demagnetize a hotter magnet. The Curie temperature thus marks a critical point at which the material makes a phase transition—from a phase in which it can hold magnetization to one in which it cannot.

In carrying forth this analogy with the cooperative phenomena of physics, it will be useful to have the concept of *hysteresis*—the phenomenon, observed in many cooperative systems, in which the local interactions are such that the change in global state of the system occurs at a point that depends on the history of the system. For example, consider using an external magnetic field in a fixed left-right direction (but the field may be either positive or negative) to reverse the magnetization of a bar magnet (figure 4.1).

Suppose that a magnetic field H_n in the positive direction is required to shift the North pole from the left to the right end of the

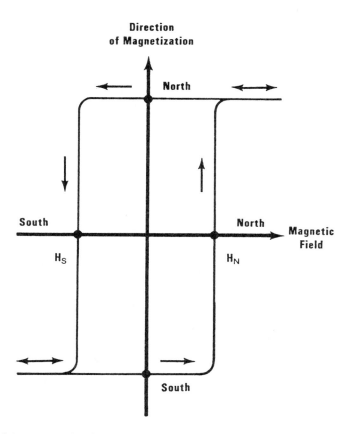

Figure 4.1 An example of a hysteresis cycle, plotting the direction of magnetization of a piece of iron against the magnitude of an external magnetic field. Because the magnetic field must flip each atomic magnet against the cooperative effect of interaction with those that remain unflipped, the field which induces a South-North transition, H_n is much larger than the reversal field, H_s.

magnet (in other words, to flip the spin of the vast majority of atomic magnets), while a magnetic field H_s is required to reverse this. Because the magnetic field does not flip each atomic magnet in isolation, but must do so against the cooperative effect of interaction with those that remain unflipped, it comes as no surprise that, at least below the Curie temperature, H_n is much larger than H_s. This, then, is how hysteresis manifests itself in magnetization. The theme to be sounded again and again in this essay is that the cooperative effect of many individuals (whether those individuals be atoms, neurons, schemas, or persons) may constitute "external forces" that make it extremely difficult for any one individual to change.

My aim here is to follow this notion of cooperative phenomena into the human sciences—to come to terms with those emergent properties, such as the ability to act, feel, and believe, which are exemplified in the human mind. We know that our brains are made up of cells called neurons, and that the complexity of a neuron is of quite a different kind from that of a mind. Can, then, a mind result from the interactions of these neurons and nothing more? Human brains differ from those of other animals; the data of the neurological clinic lead us to understand that these differences are intimately related to differences between human and animal brains, thus encouraging many neurologists to seek a physical basis for mind. Nonetheless, people can still argue as to whether humans have minds because brain evolution reached a point where the cooperative interactions of neurons yielded mental operations in and of themselves, or because the brain's very complexity led to the emergence (with or without the intervention of a primordial "whole-making" agency, be it a Deity or otherwise) of a whole, the human mind, which is novel in the sense of emergent evolutionism. The latter view is dualism.

I will outline a few cases in which the study of cooperative phenomena shows how aspects of mind can be exhibited as properties of complex interactions in neural networks. This does not prove that the dualist is wrong—it simply shows that those who reject dualism can point to a growing number of case studies consistent with their worldview. (In our book *The Construction of Reality*, Mary Hesse and I (Arbib and Hesse 1986) reach a similar conclusion. We construct a shared epistemology based on schema theory (see below), but we then show that this cannot distinguish between the voluntarist and decisionist views of free will (chapter 5), or the Christian and secular views of reality (chapters 11 and 12). What it can do is show that certain positions are consistent, while others are less so. Thus my aim in this article is to show the internal coherence of a nondualist view of the mind—and to introduce the reader to some exciting chapters of science approached in this (nondualist!) spirit—but I do not believe it is possible to refute dualism by such arguments.)

Cragg and Temperley (1954) were perhaps the first to propose a sophisticated statistical analysis of the brain by drawing analogies between cortical activity and domain formation in ferromagnets. For our present purposes, we will leave aside the discussion of temperature and instead concentrate on the point made by Cragg and Temperley: local interactions in a neural network can yield a global pattern. For example, the visual cortex contains a great variety of cells tagged not only for visual direction but also for depth in the visual field. Thus we can imagine the process of recognizing regions in the visual input at different depths to be one of suppressing all neural activity except that corresponding to the depths within a given direction—so that the process of segmentation has much in common with the domain formation that occurs in magnets.

It is in this spirit that I wish to offer a naturalist account of human minds in terms of the operation of neurons. However, the gap from mind to neuron is too large for this to be accomplished directly. We need a bridging language, and I shall offer the language of schema theory as providing that bridge. The mind can be analyzed in terms of language, vision, and so on, and these are composed of words, images, and feelings, which are themselves richly related and associated. My aim is to offer a theory in which the "units" of the mind are examples of what we shall call *schemas*. Our knowledge as individuals is embedded in a network of schemas; these schemas bridge between the descriptive levels of minds and neurons.

To give a more precise account of schema theory, we must distinguish between *external* and *internal* schemas. When we analyze a person's behavior "from the outside," we may see regularities of thought or action or custom which we may describe as constituting an "external" schema, an observable pattern of behavior. In fact, we shall extend this use of schemas from the individual to society, when we see coherent patterns of behavior emerging across the activities of the members of some society. However, when we wish to form the bridge from mind to neurons, we shall seek to see how these external schemas are the overt show of the working of "internal" schemas, the processes within the individual's head whereby action and perception are molded.

A schema may be likened to a program, but it is more like the computer program which can execute endless variations on the basis of tests of the situation than it is like the theater program which specifies step by step what is to be done, invariably. By this I do not mean to claim that human action is more like the repetitive behavior of a pre-computer (a gear-wheels and drive-belts) machine than it is like a drama. Rather, I am contrasting the flexibility of action that follows from responsiveness to endless variations of context and internal state with the fixed sequence of scenes that attends each repetition of a play. An individual's schemas are not determinants of stereotyped behavior, but are responsive to an appreciation of current circumstances to guide behavior in more or less flexible ways. With this, we can see the problems of cooperative phenomena to which we are challenged by our

consideration of "neurons, schemas, and persons." Where the cooperative phenomena of physics studies global organization in a large sys-
tem-such as the overall pattern of magnetization in a multitude of
atomic magnets, or phase transitions between relatively few phases of
matter-we must study the formation of complex mental patterns.

We are then led to ask three questions. The "downward" question: *1) How does the activity of a large population of neurons cooperate to constitute a schema?* The "upward" questions: *2) How might the
activity of a network of schemas come to constitute a personality? 3)
How does an individual acquire the schemas that constitute, or construct, such a reality?*

What Is Schema Theory?

In seeking to link mind and brain, we find it useful to distinguish two
modes of functioning: a coarse-grain style of computation distributed
across a network of relatively large subsystems, and a fine-grain style
involving parallel processing by an array of neurons. Schema theory
provides the "coarse-grain" analysis intermediate between overall
behavior and neural circuitry. A schema is the basic functional unit of
action, thought, and perception. While the main burden of this paper
is to look at the philosophical implications of the concepts of neural
networks and schemas for our understanding of person and society, let
me briefly note that the scientific background includes the study of
schemas for perception and action, and the dynamics of schema use
and change.

While the concept of the schema in Western thought goes back at
least to its use by Kant in the late 1700s, the twentieth century history
of schemas starts with the neurological study of Head and Holmes
(1911) of the postural schema. They observed the way in which the
parietal lobe of the brain subserved the individual's appreciation of his
or her body. A person with damage to the parietal lobe on one side of
the brain might actually lose awareness that the body on the opposite
side actually belonged to her. Frederick Bartlett, a student of Head,
took up the notion of schemas in his study *Remembering* (1932),
showing that people tended to remember more by relating what they
experienced to a familiar set of schemas than by rote memorization of
arbitrary details. The linkage of Kant to this modern tradition was fur-
thered by Kenneth Craik's (1943) essay *The Nature of Explanation*,
where he observed that the brain creates an internal model of the
world, allowing a person to form expectations on which actions could
be based adaptively.

Although this British tradition was quite separate from the continental tradition, we can see resonances here with Piaget's use of schemas (Piaget 1971; Beth and Piaget 1966) in his study of cognitive development in terms of *assimilation* (making sense of the situation in terms of the available stock of schemas) and *accommodation* (developing new schemas to the extent that mismatches arise). This approach to learning reminds us that much of the current excitement about neural networks—as a source not only for understanding the brain but also as a new technology—has centered on the fact that there are a number of learning rules which allow a network of neurons to adapt itself automatically to conform to some specification of its input-output behavior. What I would add to this is that behaviors are subserved by large assemblages of schemas, and so we must complement a fine-grain analysis of how a particular network can adapt itself (the study of adaptive networks) with a coarse-grain analysis of how a network of schemas may come to subserve overall behavior (the study of schema architecture). We might also note that the learning time for a network can be inordinately long unless the initial structure of the network is appropriate, and so the development of intelligence requires a balance between innate structure and ability to learn.

My own group has used schemas to provide a functional analysis of brain mechanisms of visuomotor coordination; intermediate level programs for mediating vision and touch and control of the movements of robots; and formal models of language acquisition and production. (This work is summarized in Arbib 1989, which provides copious further references to work on schemas and neural networks.) We see an assemblage of schemas as representing the current situation in which the human finds himself or herself; planning then yields a coordinated control program of motor schemas which guides our actions. To comprehend the situation we call upon tens or hundreds of schemas in our current schema assemblage, but this "short-term memory" puts together instances of schemas drawn from a long-term memory which encodes a lifetime of experience in a personal "encyclopedia" of hundreds of thousands of schemas, ranging from perceptual schemas for words and objects through memories of many specific episodes in our lives, to skills and belief systems—which themselves weave together a multitude of other schemas.

A schema, then, provides abilities for recognition and guides to action. But, as already noted in our mention of Craik, schemas must also provide expectations about what will happen so that we may choose our actions appropriately. These expectations may be wrong, and so it is that we sometimes learn from our mistakes. Learning is necessary because schemas are fallible. Schemas, and their connections within the schema network, change through the processes of accommodation. These processes adjust the network of schemas so that over time one may well be able to handle a certain range of situations in a more adaptive way. In many ways, then, these processes are reminiscent of the way in which a scientific community modifies and develops its theories on the basis of the pragmatic criterion of successful prediction and control (Hesse 1980).

While the development of the above examples of successful scientific investigations in the domain of schema theory would burden this paper unduly, it is worth stressing that our schema theory sees behavior not as based on inferences from a few simple axioms, but rather as the result of analogical reasoning based on a vast array of examples encoded in our schemas which, by the nature of our limited experience, do not constitute a completely consistent axiom-based logical system. In this framework, a schema is a unit for the construction of our representations of reality, but is more like a molecule than an atom—in that schemas may well be linked to others to provide yet more comprehensive schemas on which a maturing understanding may build. Each mind comprises a richly interconnected network of schemas, a network that brings together our notions of reality at many different levels.

With this background, we can now turn to the three questions with which we ended section 1. We will address the "downward" question ("downward" relative to the schemas within the head of an individual) in the next section, where we will see how the cooperative computation of many neurons comes to constitute a specific schema. We will then turn to the "upward" questions as we move our notion of cooperative computation up two levels, first showing how a network of schemas can cooperate to constitute a personality, and then how the schemas held by many individuals may cooperate to form a social reality—constituting what we shall call a "social schema"—which provides the context within which an individual may be socialized. We will end by noting that these social schemas are no guarantee of individual conformity. Along the way, we will note a number of challenges for the future development of schema theory if it is to provide an adequate basis for a cognitive science that addresses the reality of social processes.

How Activity of a Neural Population
Can Constitute a Schema

As one of the many possible examples of how activity of a neural population can constitute a schema, we analyze a schema for perception of motion. The visual perception of motion is far different from the subtleties of the recognition of objects in a complex and changing environment, let alone our knowledge as social beings. It must be stressed from the outset that I make no claim that all, or even many, of the schemas to be talked about in later sections have yet been explicated at the level of neural networks. However, I do wish to convince the reader that the attempt to understand the human mind in terms of interacting schemas, and the attempt to view these schemas in terms of assemblages of other schemas—with the expectation that all in the end are expressions of activity in a neural network—is indeed a reasonable program for cognitive science. Then, in later sections, I turn from this evolving account of schemas "in the head" to outline how the development of such schemas may constitute, and also be a response to, a social reality.

With this, we show how a network of neuron-like elements can compute "optic flow" as our explicit example of cooperative computation in a neural network. Each neuron in the early stages of the visual system monitors a small part of the retina—it is stimulated by activity in a relatively small part of the visual world called its receptive field. The question for our cooperative computation analysis is to understand how a global pattern emerges which unites these "visual fragments" into a confident perception of the movement of objects in the external world.

Imagine that we are watching a movie in which succeeding frames (the first frame and the second frame) are perceived as part of a pattern of continuous movements. In figure 4.2, we pose the problem in a stark way by showing a picture in which four circles indicate features of the external world as seen in the first frame of a visual sequence, while the crosses indicate the positions of the same feature in the second frame. Here we are to imagine that the external world contains four distinctive visual features which the imaging apparatus has mapped onto the four features captured in two successive frames. How are we to match the circles in the first frame with the correct crosses in the second frame, i.e., so that a first-frame feature is matched with a second-frame feature just in case they comprise successive views of the same feature of the external world? This is the *stimulus-matching* or *correspondence* problem.

In general, the world is made up of surfaces, and nearby features of the visual world are more likely to lie on the same surface than on different surfaces. For this reason we would, in general, prefer the matching which yields a relatively continuous "optic flow" (figure 4.2b) to the one with random displacements of nearby features from one frame to the next (figure 4.2a). The MATCH algorithm (Prager and Arbib 1983) is "in the style of the brain," in that it solves the stimulus-matching problem using a retinotopic array of local processors, which we shall call "neurons." (A retinotopic array is one in which the position of a neuron in the array corresponds to the position of a neuron's focal stimulation on the retina; thus neighboring neurons in the array monitor neighboring, even overlapping, portions of the visual field.) Each neuron makes an initial estimate of the optic flow based on its localized sample of the retina for the two frames. Neurons then pass messages back and forth to neighboring neurons, in an iterative process.

To understand this iterative process, we must distinguish two time scales. The "slow" time scale is that on which successive frames of visual input are introduced. But much neural activity is required to come up with the best estimate of the optic flow on the basis of the data afforded by even only two frames. Thus we must have a much faster time scale on which the neurons interact with each other. The state of each "neuron" in the array represents the current "vote" for the optic flow vector for the region of the image to which that neuron corresponds in the retinotopic array. On each iteration, all the neurons adjust their current vote through interactions with their neighbors. Many iterations may be needed to compute the optic flow for a pair of frames.

Each iteration of the MATCH algorithm makes use of two consistency conditions. The first of these is *feature matching*: to the ex-

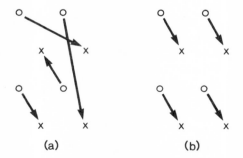

(a)   (b)

Figure 4.2 The external world contains four distinctive visual features which the imaging apparatus has mapped onto the four features captured in each of two successive frames: the four circles indicate the view of these features in the first frame of a movie, while the crosses indicate their positions in the second frame. The stimulus matching, or correspondence, problem is to match each first-frame feature with a second-frame feature just in case they comprise successive views of the same characteristic of the external world. Which of the two patterns of feature matching shown in the figure (pattern a or pattern b) is the more likely?

tent possible, the optic flow vector should carry a first-frame feature to a nearby, similar feature in the second frame. The other consistency condition is *local smoothness*. This is the condition based on the observation that the world is made up of surfaces—it states that, in general, nearby features should be displaced by similar amounts.

In figure 4.3, the current estimate for the optic flow from point A shows it as the vector leading to point B. This could be updated on the current iteration by feature matching to find the vector linking A to the feature nearest (in some combination of distance and feature type) to B in the second frame. Local smoothness could be used to find a vector which displaces A with the average displacement of its neighbors. In fact, the MATCH algorithm updates the estimate at each iteration by making the new estimate a linear combination of the feature matching update and the local-smoothness update. In computer simulations we found that twenty iterations, each of which updates all the neurons in the array, were sufficient to provide a relatively stable estimate of the optic flow.

To emphasize the need for interactions between elements to form a correct global estimate, we look at figure 4.4. Here we see the dashed circle visual field has a plausible optic flow, but even though it is plausible that optic flow estimate is based on local information which is quite at variance with the *correct* optic flow as given by rotation

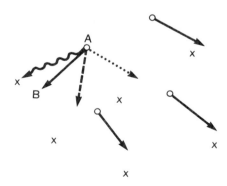

Figure 4.3 One iteration of the MATCH algorithm: The solid arrows show the current estimate of the optic flow—the head of the arrow shows the posited displacement in the second frame of the first-frame feature at the tail of the arrow. "Feature matching" alone would adjust A's optic flow to the wavy arrow pointing to the the second frame feature nearest to B (the current estimate of A's second-frame position); "local smoothness" would yield the dotted arrow, the average of the optic flow of the neighbors. The MATCH algorithm yields the dashed arrow as a weighted combination of these two estimates.

Figure 4.4 The first frame comprises the dots indicated by circles; the second frame is obtained by rotating the array about the pivot at A, to place the dots in the positions indicated by crosses. The dashed circle at lower right is the receptive field of a local processor. Solid arrows indicate the best *local* estimate of the optic flow; the dashed arrows show the actual pairing of features under rotation about A.

around the pivot point. It is only through the iterative interaction of nearby processes that eventually the global pattern is formed. This example reveals the essence of cooperative computation at the fine-grain level: parallel interaction of similar processors can yield a global pattern.

An Evolutionary Perspective

I now want to build on this example of cooperative computation at the fine-grain level to give the complementary lesson that, in general, complex behaviors will involve a coarse-grain style of computation distributed across a network of subsystems. The subsystems in the network may either be further refined in terms of other schemas, or may be directly implemented as a network of neurons. At the same time, this section will provide an evolutionary perspective which will extend our understanding of the "style of the brain."

   To get the discussion going, consider where it is that the MATCH algorithm (summarized at level 1 in figure 4.5) runs into trouble. The feature matching update seeks to match a feature in the first frame with a similar feature in the second frame. This will work well if the real-world feature is visible in both frames, but if the feature becomes either hidden or disclosed in the change of viewpoint from the first frame to the second frame, then a correct feature match will not be possible. Similarly, the local-smoothness-update is successful when the neighbors of a particular feature lie on the same surface, but this neighborhood constraint will be inappropriate if the neighbors lie on opposite sides of an edge separating two distinct objects. However, these problems provide an "evolutionary opportunity."

To find edges in the image, we can design one algorithm which will look for the breakdown of feature matching to postulate an edge, whereas a second algorithm can look for regions in which nearby points have discord in estimates of the optic flow. Then, as shown at level 2 in figure 4.5, these two algorithms can cooperate (at the coarse-grain level, constraining the fine-grain cooperative interaction within each subsystem) to come up with a confident estimate of an edge in the image.

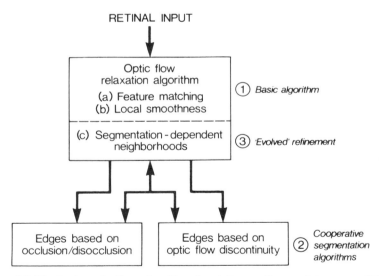

Figure 4.5 The basic optic flow algorithm (level 1) uses the consistency conditions of feature matching and local smoothness. The resultant optic flow estimates permit the hypothesizing of edges on cues based on both occlusion/disocclusion and on optic flow discontinuity (level 2). The resultant edge hypotheses can then be used to refine the computation of optic flow (level 3) by dynamically adjusting the neighborhoods used in employing the consistency conditions.

Going even further, though, the "evolution" of these edge-finding algorithms now provides the basis for the refinement of the original algorithm. We can now dynamically change the neighborhood of a point (at level 3 in figure 4.5) so that the matching of features—or the conformity with neighboring flow—can be based more on features on the same side of the currently hypothesized boundary than on features which appear to be separated. Such a refinement of the algorithm yields markedly improved performances, for instead of blurring the optic flow near an edge, it allows both the confident estimation of the position of edges, and the sharpening of the estimate of optic flow for points which appear to lie on the same object.

The design of the overall system of figure 4.5 offers what I believe to be a very important evolutionary design process. The "evolutionarily more primitive" system provides the basis for the evolution of higher level systems. But these new systems then provide an environment in which return pathways can evolve which enable the lower-level system to evolve in turn into a more effective form, i.e., one able to yield adaptive behavior in a wider set of circumstances. This exemplifies, in a computationally explicit form, the notions of the nineteenth century English neurologist Hughlings Jackson—who viewed the brain in terms of levels of increasing evolutionary complexity. In many cases, he saw damage to the brain not so much in terms of the loss of function of the damaged region but rather in terms of the release of "older" brain regions from inhibition by the damaged area, which provided controls that had evolved at a later stage of evolution. In other words, such brain damage can often be seen as revealing behavior that is more primitive in evolutionary terms. As the brain evolves, new patterns of neural activity provide new "ecological niches" for the evolution of neural circuitry to exploit these patterns. Once such new circuitry evolves, there is a new "information environment" for earlier circuitry, which may also evolve in turn so as to exploit the new patterns.

How Schemas Can Constitute a Personality

Schema theory analyzes the complexity of our minds in terms of a network of schemas—competing and cooperating to form assemblages which will control behavior, building on our current needs, motivations, and cognitive representations to actively assimilate our surroundings and determine a course of action. The MATCH algorithm provides an exemplary answer to the "downward" question of how the activity of a large population of neurons can cooperate to constitute a schema. Moreover, our account of the evolution of this algorithm shows how a network of schemas or subsystems may act together in a closely coupled way to yield an overall behavior more effective than that which any one of them can achieve alone. In a sense, then, we are already *en route* to an understanding of how we might answer the first of the "upward" questions with which we closed section 1: how might the activity of a network of schemas come to constitute a personality? Schemas that form a network within the brain of the same body have developed from a genetic structure for the growth of a single organism—and are shaped by a commonality of experience in the physical and social world. Outside the individual there is an external spatio-temporal reality of physical and biological processes independent of human constructs, as well as a "social world." Moreover, the social and nonsocial are not always clearly separable. In later sections, I shall talk more about "learning from society." Here I simply want to suggest what adaptive processes can contribute to the emergence of an individual style in a network of schemas.

Piaget's processes of assimilation and accommodation provide the engine of self-organization for the network of schemas embodied within a single brain, developing schemas of greater generality and reducing inconsistencies and creating greater coherence between schemas. However, there will also be conflicts within the network—inconsistencies will remain. To some extent we acquire a personality through our interaction with other personalities. Freud's study of the notion of identification has made clear that "role models" may create tension, as the emulation of their behavior takes us into situations that we then discover to be denied to us.

What should also be clear is that there is no single set of schemas imposed upon all persons. The uniqueness of endowment and experience yields the unique (and changing) schema network which makes each person an individual.

Large assemblages of schemas interact, compete, and cooperate to commit the organism to a relatively well integrated plan of action. However, consciousness seems to be rather focused, with only a few schemas in direct awareness at any time. At the core of our person-reality is our self-awareness and consciousness, and so we must complement the scientific theory of schemas that we have sampled above with a sketch of why it might be that we have patterns of schema activity that correlate with the phenomena of consciousness.

Our discussion of Hughlings Jackson showed that the brain so evolves that new brain regions or schemas can exploit the extant richness of the brain so that—and this is the important point—once these new systems are available, they provide a richer environment for the older ones which now have new possibilities for further evolution. We incorporate tools into our body schema. Analogously, as creatures developed as social animals, their schemas came to represent their "bodies" not as ending at the extremities of the physical body but rather as extending to incorporate aspects of other members of the group.

Our hypothesis about the evolution of consciousness (Arbib and Hesse 1986; Arbib 1985) starts with the notion that out of the needs of group communication evolved the ability to form a précis of schema activity to serve as the basis for the control of nonverbal communication to enable group members to coordinate better with one another. It is important to note that there is no claim that, at the earliest stages of its evolution, such a précis plays any role in deciding what to do next. However, in our "Jacksonian" terms, we can see that once the précis is available as part of the way the brain has evolved, older patterns of schema interaction may become modified in turn. There are occasions on which they can be better coordinated via the précis, and thus it would come about that the précis would develop into a subnetwork (not necessarily localized) with bidirectional links into the schema network, and that this subnetwork would then evolve to have a role that is sometimes directive. The full development of these ideas will take us some way into situating some of Freud's insights about the unconscious in terms of our modern schema theory.

This evolutionary process sets the stage both for consciousness and for the evolution of language to express this précis of the richness of schema activity. We may distinguish the explicit effects of schema interaction from the more highly evolved effects of the conscious use of language, and note that there is no necessary congruence between them. A person may hold a belief contrary to what she admits to believing. For example, if she says she believes in the importance of politics yet never votes, her belief in the unimportance of politics is tacit in her conduct even though she has not acknowledged that she holds this belief. If she finally admits to the evidence of her behavior, this belief becomes explicit but is still incomplete. She must not only see that the belief is embodied in her behavior but must also endorse it or reject it and reshape her behavior accordingly. To hold a belief is not only to act on it but also to be able to give reasons to support it and to understand the circumstances in which it might be revised. With this we see not only how schemas can constitute personality and how, in some sense, that personality may be unitary, but that the competition and cooperation among schemas, and coherences and conflicts within the development of a schema network, provide plenty of room for understanding those diversities which each of us discover within ourselves—no matter how happily integrated we may normally consider ourselves to be.

Social Schemas

We have pursued our theme of cooperative computation into the human sciences at ever higher levels, looking first at how the activity of neurons may cooperate to constitute a schema, and then how the activity of schemas (whether conscious or unconscious) may cooperate to constitute a personality. We now turn to the question of how the activity of a population of people can cohere to constitute a society. However, I am not concerned with giving a Rousseau-esque story of how the Social Contract might originally have been formed, but rather with looking at how it is—and this was the second of our "upward" questions at the end of section 1—that the individual becomes a member of an existing society, acquiring the schemas that constitute, or construct, a social reality. I shall then turn to the issue of how it is that, while many individuals may come to be integrated members of a community, the path of dissent is still open for others.

The driving force for the questions that I raise in the rest of the paper comes from the work that Mary Hesse and I did in preparing ourselves for our Gifford lectures in natural theology at the University of Edinburgh in 1983, since published as *The Construction of Reality* (Arbib and Hesse 1986). I came to this work with a background in understanding how schemas might be implemented in terms of neural networks in the brain, or as programs in the controllers of robots. For me, schemas were in the head of the individual, be it robot, animal, or human. By contrast, Mary Hesse came to our joint enterprise from a background in philosophy of science. The analog of a schema for her was a scientific theory—or some other social construct such as a religion, language, or ideology. To bridge between our two concerns one might phrase the questions of the history of science as follows: How is it that the schemas in the heads of individual scientists may cooperate to yield a "phase transition" which leads to the establishment of a new scientific theory? Here we go from an account of individual creativity to the creation of patterns of broad agreement across a group of scholars. This in turn leads to the question of how we may relate the notion of a schema as something in the head with the view of a schema as a theory or ideology or religion—as something which is rather the expression of a community. It is to the elucidation of these questions that the rest of this paper is devoted. Needless to say, much of what follows is heavily influenced by my collaboration with Mary

Hesse. Let us, then, return to our specific question: How does the individual acquire the schemas that constitute, or construct, a social reality? In other words, how can the process of socialization be related to the process of schema change within the individual?

We learn from "society" because we interact with individuals who, already being members of the community, provide patterns of behavior which exhibit regularities that transcend the idiosyncrasies of any one individual (these idiosyncrasies may themselves be accommodated by schemas which represent individuals or the roles of such individuals). These patterns are exhibited by the society *en masse* and so constitute an external reality that allows the child to develop schemas to internalize the community. We shall speak of *social schemas*— networks of interaction among the individuals of a society, their institutions and artifacts—to distinguish these patterns from the schemas held in the head of the individual. These are thus akin to Durkheim's (1938) "collective representations." Such schemas shape the development of the individual's many internal schemas at least as powerfully as patterns of physical reality shape the development of sensorimotor schemas. Social schemas are holistic, though not necessarily monolithic, nets of social reality, of custom, language, and religion. Clearly, such a network may not exist independent of individuals and their mental schemas, and yet cannot be fully represented within the head of any one individual.

Schemas may find their full meanings only in terms of the network of which they are a part. Such networks may unite schemas in the head with social schemas and aspects of the world itself. In particular, it is not necessary that all details of an individual's interaction with the world be fully codified within a schema within her own brain. Much of memory is external. In computer terms: we do not need to store a complete program which explicitly describes every contingency if we can generate behavior in interaction with cues provided by the external world. In terms of everyday experience, we may not be able to recall every detail of the way from home to our workplace—it suffices that, at the sight of a familiar landmark, we may then recall which way to turn. In the same way, our behavior as members of a society may involve the use of legal texts, religious writings, and rituals performed with others. Such artifacts and performances may crystallize social schemas into forms that increase their repeatability from individual to individual, but they are no guarantee that every individual will conform, or that any individual will conform all of the time. Some codifications always remain in tension with the dynamism of individuals within the greater society, as I emphasize in the next section.

Ideology and Revolt

We have come to see that schemas are both in heads and in the social relations among heads. This is perhaps most clearly exemplified in thinking of language both as a social reality external to the individual and as an "idiolect" internalized in the schemas of each individual, so that the language community is constituted by the schemas of many individuals. A similar dichotomy may be seen in approaches to the study of society and ideology (Connolly 1981). A top-down or structuralist view conceives the relations of the members of society as determined by the roles (or the class) they occupy and the forces impinging on such roles at the level of social structures. In contrast, a bottom-up or interpretive view stresses the schemas that an individual has constructed in internalizing social roles, focusing on the intersubjective dimension acquired through growing up with others in a particular society.

We have used schema theory to develop an interpretive view of the individual in society. However, the notion of cooperative phenomena clarifies how it is that the patterns of individual schemas may cohere into an external social schema which provides a psychically tangible external reality to individuals in that society. As individuals accommodate to communal patterns they provide part of the coherent context for others. But we have also seen that the uniqueness of both genetic endowment and individual experience ensures that no two members of a society have the exact same individual schemas in their head, and so the commonality of social behaviors still leaves space for discord. The individual can shape schemas that not only enable the playing of various roles, but also provide a critique that may emerge in overt dissent. The attainment of coherent internalizations of social schemas may entail that people share understandings of social relationships and that their behavior may be conditioned by their appreciation of what social roles are open to them, but does not entail identical patterns of behavior in different individuals. Accommodation to a perceived social role may constrain an individual's behavior, but will not completely determine it.

The dynamics of individual change can be greatly constrained by the inertia of a whole population. Mass hysteria can sweep up individuals into patterns of change they would reject in a framework of individual consideration. More generally, once a social system is in place, it is difficult for people to act outside it, even if they conclude that it is unjust or question the efficacy of certain rituals. In particular, state power, control of labor, or threats of ostracism penalize those who overtly question ideology. If the chance of punishment outweighs the expectation of reform, individuals may come to repress their dissident thoughts. Note that this talk of state power shows that schema theory needs the structural level of analysis to see how individual schemas become "crystallized" in institutions with rules that become in no small part constitutive of personal reality. We are again reminded of how the theory of cooperative phenomena shows how the interaction of local forces may cohere to provide global forces which may be seen as in some sense determinative of much of individual activity. Just as it is hard to reverse the magnetization of a magnet through local changes of the magnetic field, so it is hard for the individual in society to maintain a marked discrepancy between role aspiration and role actuality.

We begin to see why it is that individuals may internalize an ideology even if it is contrary to what they might themselves come up with in their own unconstrained critique. We do not come to society "from outside" with schemas that may be used for a rational critique free of social preconceptions. Rather, we grow up in a society, accommodating our schemas to assimilate social norms and standards of language and logic in a richly interconnected network that has no prespecified boundaries. Thus the grounds for critique may not (at least initially) even be perceptible in terms of the internal schemas which have accommodated the regnant social schemas of the community. Yet the very dynamics of individual schema change may lead to a discord between an individual's schemas and the social schemas around her, and the result may indeed be a critique of those social schemas. This notion of "critique" reminds us that a schema-based psychology requires not simply the schemas that locate us in the here and now of the present situation but the ability to imagine alternatives— conceiving of things as other than they are, and as better (note the evaluative dimension here). In fact, even the most elementary forms of artificial intelligence must, at the minimum, search a tree of possible courses of action to determine the one that is best or, given the constraints of time available before action must be taken, the one that is most satisfactory among those considered. What we are asking for now is a metalevel of analysis, in which the search is not so much among courses of action as it is among belief structures and evaluation criteria, seeking schemas which can better accommodate the appearances of a complex world.

But the apparent utility of such changed schemas to an individual (whether or not they can be consciously articulated) is no guarantee of their wider acceptance. An individual may share her critique with a small circle of family, friends, or acquaintances, but a social critique elaborated by a small group of individuals often becomes repressed or remains restricted to discussions within that small group. Only in exceptional cases will a critique spread to the point of effecting an enduring restructuring of society. Again, the study of a cooperative phenomenon gives us analogies which illuminate what is going on here. Consider a seed-crystal being dropped into a supersaturated solution which then suddenly crystallizes. For most temperatures and concentrations of material within the solution, the dropping of the seed would have no marked effect. We have to understand what it is about the solution—the seed's "environment"—which makes it subject to sudden change. Social change requires dissatisfaction, mobilization, publicity—and a critical mass of people for whom the new schemas "make sense." Thus our understanding of social change remains inextricably linked to our understanding of the dynamics of an individual's schemas. We have much to learn about what it is that makes an overtly presented system of ideas more or less accommodatable within a given network of individually held schemas.

Here we can apply the vocabulary of the mathematical analysis of dynamical systems, talking of structural stability and bifurcations. In most states of a system a small change—to the action of any one individual in a social system—will only result in a small effect. But there is a relatively small set of situations in which a small change can be magnified to cause the overall system to effect a phase transition from one overall mode of behavior to a qualitatively differently one. Such a change may be referred to as a bifurcation, from one regime of structural stability to another (see the companion paper by Peacocke, this volume). In the same way, only in certain situations may an individual critique become widely accepted, irrespective of its intrinsic merits—even though it is individual beliefs that in their cooperativity constitute the regnant social schemas. The individual cannot be effective without a certain social stage, but the stage is bare without the actors.

And again, from what perspective may the intrinsic merits of beliefs be judged? For example, Arbib and Hesse 1986 (see especially the last two chapters) find that the epistemology of schema theory is neutral between a secular social schema and the "Great Schema" of the Bible, no matter how strongly one may argue for either on the basis of one's individual life—experience as encapsulated in one's internal schemas. Incidentally, this last observation makes clear that the people within a geographical region are by no means restricted to a homogeneous set of social schemas. Neighbors may differ as to occupation, religion, and political preference. Dually, since an individual's perception of a social schema is rooted in her sampling of that schema from its individual expression in books, artifacts, and people's behavior, we

may see why it is that two members of the same church or political
party may differ so drastically in their understanding of what that alle-
giance entails. There is thus much subtlety in trying to understand
where the line is crossed from acceptable variations to differences that
are felt to threaten the social fabric—as in understanding whether the
difference in two political views is or is not containable within the limits of distribution of power within a democracy.

Leaving aside these large-scale issues, however, I want to return
to the distinction between explicit and implicit schemas that we
looked at earlier (as where apolitical behavior implicitly refuted explicit contrary claims). Explicit critique may occupy the intellectual,
yet at most it provides—via the media and bar-room debates—
implicit grist for the mill of schema accommodation and schema assimilation by "the general public." Few, if any, conclusions are
reached by purely deductive analysis from well-founded axioms. We
act on feelings of commitment that may be based more on tacit
knowledge (activation of schemas embodying related experiences)
than on verbal analysis. We may entertain an inchoate set of possibilities and be forced to "leap" before we have had time for thoughtful reflection on them. Even to the extent that we, as adults, develop skills
for logical analysis, too much of our argument is rooted in tacit networks of schemas for our critique of society to be entirely free of the
social schemas that constitute it. But whether based on explicit reasoning or not, such critiques may, sometimes, yield radical changes in
overt behavior.

Most people want some congruence between hopes and aspirations and their actual life situations. Few people build their lives
around striving for a goal if its attainment appears unlikely—though
many forms of religious belief show that the goal need not appear
likely of attainment in this life. For most people, dreams are soon discarded as the stuff of adolescence. A goal is to be striven for only if it
appears likely of attainment; otherwise one's goals and aspirations
should themselves be adjusted into congruence with reality. We have
seen that a schema may be considered in two senses, either as
"external" or "internal." The external dimension can provide intersub-
jectivity; the further the underlying schema develops in isolation, the
more difficult it is to communicate about it and the less likely it is that
it will ever play a socially effective role, even if it comes to dominate
the thinking of the person who nurtured it. In some cases—religious
fanatic or the confirmed revolutionary—the interiorization of the
"socially aberrant" is so great that it constitutes the believer's reality.
The feedback that signals a discrepancy does not say which—belief or
society—must be changed to reduce it.

Conclusion

We have seen how to link the physical theory of cooperative phenomena and the neurobiological/psychological theory of neurons and schemas with a number of social concerns. I have argued that cooperative computation provides us with the beginning of a theory of stable states of schemas within the individual's head and stable states of schemas within society.

The study of optic flow gave a sample answer to the downward question of how the activity of a large population of neurons can cooperate to constitute a schema. The evolutionary view of the optic flow algorithm and the preliminary theory of consciousness augment Piagetian ideas of assimilation and accommodation to give some sense of how activity of a network of schemas may come to constitute a personality. But just as the Freudian analysis of identification reminded us that there can be conflicts as well as coherence within the schemas within the head of an individual, so we have seen that there can be coherence and conflict within the network of schemas that constitute a society.

In many ways the networks of schemas possessed in the heads of individuals may yield commonalities of external behavior which provide the regularities—call them social schemas or collective representations—which can drive the accommodation of schemas that a child makes as she joins her society. Yet the uniqueness of the individual's genetic endowment and experience can still provide the diversity of individual schemas which can lead individuals to make a critique of their society. With this understanding of the interaction between individual and social schemas we can integrate the structuralist and interpretive views of society within our language of cooperative computation: the cooperative interactions of individual schemas may form an almost unbudgeable social reality; yet there are nonetheless limited circumstances, analogous to the state of a saturated solution, in which society can be responsive to the effect of individual actions in triggering massive social changes. Whether one wishes to say that it is the individual or the set of social circumstances that is the cause of the change is more a matter of personal temperament than of scientific objectivity, for neither can act effectively without the other.

Note added in proof: The events in Eastern Europe at the end of 1989 provide rich examples of the operation of processes such as those that have been the theme of this paper.

ACKNOWLEDGEMENTS

I wish to thank Joe Earley, who arranged the Georgetown Conference, did much to aid in the preparation of the paper, and contributed immensely to the intellectual liveliness of the meeting. My thanks also to Jack Crossley, Louis Dupré, Walter Fisher, and Frederick Ferré for their constructive criticism of an earlier draft.

REFERENCES

Arbib, M. A. 1985. *In Search of the Person: Philosophical Explorations in Cognitive Science*. Amherst: University of Massachusetts Press.

Arbib, M. A. 1989. *The Metaphorical Brain 2: Neural Networks and Beyond*. New York: Wiley-Interscience.

Arbib, M. A., and M. B. Hesse. 1986. *The Construction of Reality*. Cambridge: Cambridge University Press.

Bartlett, F. C. 1932. *Remembering*. Cambridge: Cambridge University Press.

Beth, E. W., and J. Piaget. 1966. *Mathematical Epistemology and Psychology* (translated from the French by W. Mays). New York: Reidel.

Connolly, W. E. 1981. *Appearance and Reality in Politics*. Cambridge: Cambridge University Press.

Cragg, B. G., and H. N. V. Temperley. 1954. "The Organization of Neurones: A Cooperative Analogy." *EEG Clin. Neurophysiol.* 6: 85-92.

Craik, K. J. W. 1943. *The Nature of Explanation*. Cambridge: Cambridge University Press.

Durkheim, E. 1938. *The Rules of Sociological Method* (S. A. Solovay and J. H. Mueller, trans.), New York: Collier-MacmMillan.

Goudge, T. A. 1967. "Emergent Evolutionism," in *The Encyclopedia of Philosophy* (P. Edwards, ed.). New York: Macmillan. 474-77.

Head, H., and G. Holmes. 1911. "Sensory Disturbances from Cerebral Lesions." *Brain* 34: 102-254.

Hesse, M. B. 1980. "Theory and Value in the Social Sciences," in *Revolutions and Reconstructions in the Philosophy of Science*. Bloomington: Indiana University Press 187-205.

Jackson, J. H. 1878-79. "On Affections of Speech from Disease of the Brain," *Brain* 1: 304-30, 2: 203-22, 323-56.

Prager, J. M., and M. A. Arbib. 1983. "Computing the Optic Flow: The MATCH Algorithm and Prediction," *Comp. Vision, Graphics and Image Proc.* 24: 271-304.

Piaget, J. 1971. *Biology and Knowledge*. Edinburgh: Edinburgh University Press.

4 : 2

DIVERSITY FROM UNITY

Murray Bowen

Psychiatrists and their institutions are generally mainly concerned with treating pathologies in patients with problems—rather than in developing theories. I have been trying to move Freudian psychiatric theory in the direction of becoming a science ever since I joined the Menninger Clinic as a psychiatric resident in 1946.

Freud intended to found a science; he was a neurologist who listened carefully as chronically neurotic patients freely associated—that is, talked at length about their life problems. He discovered that they related to him with the same relationship patterns they had used with their parents and with other people important in their lives. This led to his definition of "transference" as a normal and healthy process. However, he found that if the analyst responded to the patient with his own feelings ("countertransference"), the analysis, or the psychotherapy, could be seriously damaged. This was a workable two-person theory, but a long way from science. Well-known science writers such as Isaac Asimov[1] believed that there would never be a science of human behavior.

Beginning in 1948, I attempted to make a combination of the theory of biological evolution and psychiatric theory, using some form of systems-theory to mediate. Neither of the two systems-theories that were then available (that of Bertalanfly[2] or that of Weiner[3]) was adequate to the job; they tended to focus primarily on the inanimate, controlled by the human. My basic approach has been to consider individual and family-group human functioning as products of biological evolution. A kind of magical change took place in my thinking when concepts of biological evolution were integrated with a small amount of psychiatric theory.

My clinical experience with severely disturbed patients, especially schizophrenics, led me to the conclusion that symptoms displayed

by one member of a family were connected in complex ways with behaviors of other members of the family, including members of past
generations, persons long dead. In the 1950s two ideas growing out of
clinical work were incorporated into the theory. One was "differentiation of self," which describes how people develop differences from
each other through multigenerational interactions. The second was
"the emotional system," which estimates the degree of attachment of a
person to others, and makes predictions of future directions of a life, as
well as giving some understanding of the present and of the past.

"Poorly differentiated" people regulate their actions largely in
terms of reactions to others (such as other members of their family);
poorly differentiated people are most likely to develop troublesome
symptoms in life's crises. In contrast, "well-differentiated" people
automatically assume normal and symptom-free life postures. A
person's level of differentiation is largely fixed by the time the person
becomes an adult, but the theory suggests ways for strongly motivated
adults to increase differentiation a bit. Increase in differentiation results in improved functioning, which is automatically healthy for a
family.

After the initial formulation of this new theory, my own functioning improved markedly. The treatment programs also did very
well, as effort was increased to have families visit often and to be
active in treatment planning. Both patients and their families were
attracted to a broad way of thinking that was impersonal, and did not
blame anyone. The theory was communicated in brief responses—
rather than in words telling patients, or their families, what to do.
Many psychotherapists have not appreciated the difference between
my approach and others; some considered my theory to be more
Freudian than it is, others considered it as a theory dealing mainly
with individuals rather than as a family-system theory.

It soon became clear that further development of theory would
require full-time research. In 1954, I moved to NIH and conducted an
extensive research program involving schizophrenics and their families. In 1959, after completion of that research, I moved to Georgetown
University and applied insights gained in work with severely impaired
patients and their families, to teaching, research, and therapy dealing
with less severe symptoms in normal individuals and families. The
theory remained intact, but continued to develop and to be extended in
various ways. In recent years, an administrative approach has been developed from the theory, and the theory has been extended to apply to
other organizational systems in addition to the family. The main points
of "Bowen Family Systems Theory" are summarized elsewhere.[*]

One of the most popular and influential aspects of the theory has been the study of differentiation within one's own family. Every human infant starts life fully dependent on others, specifically on the family of origin. Growing up involves progressive development of individual characteristics, and aspects of increasing independence. The development of self occurs, in the case of each person, in and through networks of relationships with other members of the family system. As Freud discovered, two-person relationships (transference-counter-transference) are important, but three-person relationships ("triangles") are the basic and relatively stable components of emotional systems of families. In many families, individual differentiation is relatively low—members generally act *in reaction* to actions, words, or wishes of others. This may work well enough in good times, but tends to develop troublesome symptoms under stress. In families in which individual members are more highly differentiated, each acts on the basis of good reasons—rather than in response to wishes or actions of other family members. A family consisting of well-differentiated persons tends to function well, even under stress.

An example may serve to illustrate the main point. In our society, spouses tend to fight each other over such issues as money, jobs, social position, academic prowess, and so on. When spouses compete with each other, their children tend to become less mature, and the marriage may end in divorce. This occurs when each spouse tends to focus on what *the other* is doing. In my view, the *differences* between spouses can provide the basis of stable marriages. Marriage is a "togetherness," but it operates best when each partner operates from within self—rather than in reaction to the other. When each is well differentiated, the man does the best he can, and the woman does the best she can; neither is dependent on the other for major decisions. The differences between the spouses complement each other; neither spouse regulates their development so as to become what the other wishes. They no longer look to each other, or to some outside source of advice, for cues as to how they should regulate their actions.

Although each spouse is caught up in togetherness at marriage, the marriage tends to be more secure when each spouse can be a self, acting from motives that arise from within self. When parents are well differentiated, the children are confident which parent is which, and they in turn tend to become more highly differentiated, and more secure, people. When each member of the family can act as a self, from self, the functioning of the family, as a unitary whole, is improved. But the development, as selves, of the children born into that family depends on the emotional system of that family. Only if the family functions well can the children develop as selves. *Out of unity* (of the family) *comes diversity* (individuality).

REFERENCES

1.   Isaac Asimov, "Lost in Space," *Discover* 9.1 (19 January 1988), 18-20.

2.   Ludwig von Bertalanfly, *General Systems Theory* (New York: George Braziller 1968).

3.   Norbert Weiner, *Cybernetics, or Control and Communication in the Animal and Machine* (New York: Wiley 1948).

4.   Murray Bowen, *Family Therapy in Clinical Practice* (New York: Jason Aronson 1978); Michael E. Kerr and Murray Bowen, *Family Evaluation* (New York: W.W. Norton 1988); Michael E. Kerr, "Darwin to Freud to Bowen," in *Georgetown Magazine* (Washington, D.C.: Georgetown University), 21.2 (Spring 1989): 17-19, 44-45.

5 : 1

NATURAL BEING AND BECOMING
—THE CHRYSALIS OF THE HUMAN

Arthur R. Peacocke

John Donne, the English divine and poet, writing in 1611, half a century or so after Copernicus' *De Revolutionibus*, could expound his *Anatomie of the World* thus:

> And new Philosophy calls all in doubt,
> The Element of fire is quite put out;
> The Sun is lost, and th'earth, and no mans
> wit
> Can well direct him where to looke for it.
> And freely men confesse that this world's
> spent,
> When in the Planets, and the Firmament
> They seeke so many new; then see that this
> Is crumbled out againe to his Atomies.

Here we sense something of that anguish which was experienced with the breakdown of the medieval perception of a divinely ordered and hierarchically organized cosmos in which humanity had an intermediate but highly significant location as a bridge between the earthly and the heavenly. We hear an echo of the desolation that was felt at the loss of an awareness of organic unity—"'Tis all in pieces"—of a divine placement for humanity, and indeed of all things living and nonliving, in an organic whole.

The roots of this organicism, including a distinctive role for humanity, can be traced back to the Greeks and Romans and found expression too in the Christian concept of the church as the "body," the *soma*, of Christ.

But neither Scripture nor the poets could stem the tide of a rising individualism in which the self surveyed the world as subject over against object. This way of viewing the world involved an abstracting in which the entities and processes of the world were broken down into their constituent units, which were conceived as wholes in themselves, whose lawlike relations it was the task of the "new philosophy" (what we call "science") to discover.

The triumphs of this approach in mechanics and astronomy that we associate with Newton and his successors established it as the normative way of questioning the natural world. It may be depicted, somewhat oversuccintly, as the asking of "What's there?"; then, "What are the relations between what is there?"; and, the ultimate objective, "What are the laws describing these relations?"

To implement this aim a *methodologically* reductionist approach was essential, especially when studying the complexities of matter (chemistry) and of living organisms (biology). The natural world studied by an increasingly detached "objective" observer came to be described as a world of entities involved in lawlike relations which determined the course of events in time. The staggering success of these procedures cannot be overestimated. In the course of three hundred years they have altered the whole perspective of Western humanity so that the historian Herbert Butterfield, in his introduction to some Cambridge lectures in 1948, could declare that

> Since that [scientific] revolution overturned the authority in science not only of the middle ages but of the ancient world....it outshines everything since the rise of Christianity and reduces the Renaisssance and the Reformation to the rank of mere episodes, mere internal displacements, within the system of medieval Christendom. Since it changed the character of men's habitual mental operations even in the conduct of the non-material sciences, while transforming the whole diagram of the physical universe and the very texture if human life itself, it looms so large as the real origin both of the modern world and of the modern mentality that our customary periodisation of European history has become an anachronism and an encumbrance.[2]

The success of the methodologically reductionist procedures of this natural science has continued to the present day, in spite of the revolution in our epistemology of the physics of the sub-atomic world that has been necessitated by the advent of quantum theory. For at the macroscopic level that is the focus of most of the sciences from chemistry to population genetics, the unpredictabilities inherent in the Heisenberg Uncertainty Principle are ironed out in the statistical certainties of the behavior of either large populations of small entities or (what often comes to the same thing) simply by the entities under examination themselves being large so that the quantum uncertainties are negligible. Predictability was expected in such macroscopic systems and, by and large, it became possible after due scientific investigation—or so it has seemed until the last few decades. For it has turned out that science, being the art of the soluble (to use Medawar's phrase), has concentrated on those phenomena most amenable to such lawlike and deterministic interpretations. What I intend to point to are some developments from within the sciences themselves that are beginning to change our perspective on the natural world in a manner that promises to allow for a coherent "placement" of human beings, with their distinctive qualities and activities, in the natural order.

Such a taking seriously of developments in the sciences involves both particular assumptions concerning their reliability—that they are not just ephemeral speculations that may pass away tomorrow—and a general conviction concerning the status of scientific affirmations. As regards the former, I can but exercise my judgment, in the confidence that fellow-scientists will be quick to point out where the ice is thin! As regards the latter, I shall be adopting a realist view of scientific propositions which is not "naive," but critical and qualified. It is realist in the sense of Jarrett Leplin, namely, that

> What realists... share in common are the convictions that scientific change is, on balance, progressive and that science makes possible knowledge of the world beyond its accessible, empirical manifestations.[3]

Science is aiming to depict reality. It is "critical" and "qualified" in the sense that it recognizes that the language of science is necessarily both metaphorical and reviseable and is shaped by continuous development in continuing linguistic communities. As Ernan McMullin has put it,

> The basic claim made by [such a critical] scientific realism...is that the long-term success of a scientific theory gives reason to believe that something like the entities and structure postulated by the theory actually exists.[4]

During the last two centuries, sciences such as chemistry, cell biology and geology, to name only a typical few, have progressively and continuously discovered hidden structures and processes in the natural world that account causally for observed phenomena. We can with some confidence, therefore, now examine certain general features of the scientific account of the world and assess their general import—with the ironic outcome, as we shall see, that some of these features call into question our ability to ascertain "causes" in and to predict the future of certain kinds of far from uncommon systems. So what do the sciences tell us is there in the world?

By far the greater proportion of the sciences are concerned with that region that lies bewteen the subatomic and the cosmological and it is in this range that a visitor to Earth from, say, some other inhabited planet would be struck by the enormous diversity of the structures and entities that exist on our planet, both living and nonliving. But, were he/she/it scientifically informed, this visitor would soon realize that this rich complexity can be seen as a diversity-in-unity wherein relatively simple laws, principles, and relationships weave, through their operation over long periods of time, the almost extravagantly rich tapestry of our world on the basis of the givenness of certain fundamental parameters (the speed of light, mass and charge of elementary particles, fundamental force interaction constants, etc.). Furthermore, the sciences of the twentieth century (let us forget our visitor now) show that these diverse organizations of matter constitute a complex hierarchy of levels, in which each successive member in a series is a "whole" constituted by an organization of "parts" preceding it in the series. Think of the sequence: atom—molecule—macromolecule—subcellular organelle—cell—multicellular organ—whole living organism—a population of organisms—an ecosystem. This is not the only kind of "hierarchy"—some exhibit relations between functions, rather than the spatial inclusion, like a set of Russian dolls, of the series just instanced. We have to take seriously this picture of the world from the natural sciences as a complex hierarchy of complexities, with each "level" usually having a corresponding science for which it is the principal focus.

Now it is a natural transition for, say, a molecular biologist who is accustomed to breaking down complex (biological) entities into units small enough to be examined by the techniques of that discipline, to transform this practical, *methodological* necessity into a more general philosophical belief that (in this case) biological organisms *are* "nothing but" the bits into which they have been analyzed (in this instance, atoms and molecules). A strong case can in fact be made that there are concepts applicable to the more complex ("higher," for brevity) levels which are not logically reducible to the concepts applicable to and appropriate for the lower levels. For example, in no way can "biological information," the *concept* of conveying a biologically significant message (concepts from communication theory) be articulated in terms of the *concepts* of physics and chemistry, even though the latter can now be shown to explain how the molecular machinery (DNA, RNA, the appropriate enzymes, etc.) operates to convey information. Thus, at the initiating point of the twentieth century revolution in biology—the discovery in 1953 of a structure of DNA that could convey biological information—we find this latter new concept being required to understand the higher level system, the DNA operating in the milieu of an evolved, living cell or organism. For such reasons many biologists have argued against "take-over" bids by molecular biologists (such as Francis Crick's "the ultimate aim of the modern movement in biology is in fact to explain *all* biology in terms of physics and chemistry");[5] anthropologists against biologists; psychologists against neurophysiologists, etc.!

Such an *epistemological* antireductionism does have some *ontological* implications for a critical realist. The concepts, if well established as required to refer to the higher level system in question, are, no doubt qualifiedly and reviseably, nevertheless attempting to depict realities at that higher level. Because of widely pervasive reductionist presuppositions, there has been a tendency to regard the level of atoms and molecules as alone being "real." But there is no sense in which subatomic particles or atoms are to be graded as "more real" than, say, a bacterial cell or a human person or a social or cultural fact. Each level has to be regarded as a slice, as it were, through the totality of reality—that which we cannot avoid taking account of in our interactions with and reflections on the world. So terms such as "consciousness," "person," "society," and, in general, the languages of the humanities, ethics, the arts, and theology—to name but a few—are not prematurely to be dismissed from the vocabulary used to describe all-that-is in the world, for in these instances a strong case can be made for the distinctiveness and nonreducibility of the concepts employed. This is not, of course, to say that in using such terms we already know all we want to know about them: such a term is used to *refer* to a reality which is only fallibly depicted in metaphor and model, without our ever being able to presume we know what it is "in itself," any more than we do in the case of subatomic particles.

So far we have been taking a rather static scientific view of the world; but scientists also address themselves to the question "What's going on?"—a question about the processes of the world. All observable entities in the world are subject to change, albeit on widely disparate time-scales, so that all "being" is in fact in process of "becoming." As is well known, time in classical physics may be reversed without changing the applicability of the laws governing motion. But, from the discovery of geological time in the eighteenth century, through the nineteenth century's major discoveries (of biological evolution, and the second law of thermodynamics and irreversibility) to our current recognition of the universe as having a beginning in the "hot big bang," the "time" with which scientists have to deal has been regarded as having a direction. And this direction is one, moreover, that seems to run parallel to that of our own consciousness. So we seek explanations of past changes in order to understand the present and, moreover, hope to be able to predict changes with time in the entities and systems of the world.

The notions of explanation of the present by examination of the past and predictability of the future are closely interlocked with the concept of causality (which, incidentally, is not vitiated by relativity theory, for the succession of events in causal chains is independent of the choice of frame of reference). "Causality" is explicated in terms of lawlike relations, if not in single causal chains, and any system for which these have been ascertained would seem *ipso facto* to be predictable. This was achieved for a number of relatively simple, dynamic systems which ranged from the movements of the planets round the Sun, to the fall and motion of bodies on the Earth, including the swing of pendula subtending only low angles. It was this ability to predict that so impressed the contemporaries of Newton—and indeed their successors for three centuries, not excluding ourselves who have seen men landed on the moon, with a precision of seconds after immense journeys, by application of this same Newtonian mechanics. In spite of its applicabiltiy to only a very restricted subset of natural phenomena, the sheer intellectual power and beauty of the Newtonian scheme led to domination both of the criterion of predictability as that which characterized successful science and of a view of the world of nature as mechanistic and deterministic. As is well known, this determinism was encapsulated in the statement of Laplace in his *Essai philosophique sur les probabilités* (1776) that "an intelligence which at any given instance comprehends all the relations of the entities of this universe,... could state the respective positions, motions and general affects of all these entities at any given time in the past or future."

The underlying basis of this schema did, of course, undergo a devastating blow with the advent of quantum theory and the realization that certain pairs of quantities (e.g.,position and velocity) characterizing the properties of subatomic particles could never both be determined with complete accuracy (the Heisenberg Uncertainty Principle). Even so, the relative uncertainties were not large for systems greater than the atomic: and the probabilities of such particles evidencing particular values of some variables could be ascertained so that the behavior of assemblies of large numbers of, say, radioactive atoms could be predicted with respect, for example, to the time it would take for half of them to break up radioactively. So in practice the advent of quantum theory did not deter scientists concerned with large numbers of constituent entities or with larger sizes than the subatomic from continuing to make deterministic assumptions and from aiming to ascertain the "laws" controlling the systems with which they were concerned.

For it was in this way that science had apparently successfully reduced the apparent "chaos" (defined, in this context, as "the state of utter confusion and disorder" (O.E.D.)) of the natural world to an orderly "cosmos" ("the world or universe as an ordered system; ...a harmonious system," O.E.D.) The whole operation, it was widely thought, increasingly allowed predictability, in principle, at the—vastly preponderant—macroscopic levels beyond those where quantum uncertainties operated. Total macroscopic predictability seemed to be attainable: that, at least, was the ostensible aim. We can now see that it was only a very selected subset of natural phenomena that were actually being successfully subsumed in this program. In the last two decades we have increasingly learned to recognize the existence of systems for which it is the case that, although simple deterministic laws control the behavior of their constituents, their macroscopic behavior as systems is, in principle and provably, not predictable—or, at least only partially so. And these systems are far from esoteric—they include the weather, the dripping of water from a tap (faucet) and the upward convection of a liquid heated from below! It now turns out that simple, deterministic laws operating at one level in a system can produce apparently random behavior in the system as a whole, so that order breeds its own kind of "chaos," a word that now has a special mathematical connotation, to be distinguished from the ordinary usage of the dictionary definition above. As James Crutchfield et al. have put it,

> ...simple deterministic systems with only a few elements can generate random behavior. The randomness is fundamental; gathering more information does not make it go away. Randomness generated in this way has come to be called chaos. A seeming paradox is that chaos is deterministic, generated by fixed rules that do not themselves involve any element of chance...small uncertainties are amplified, so that even though the behavior is predictable in the short term, it is unpredictable in the long term.[6]

So, paradoxically, we now have to accept *both* that the uncertainities and randomness at a microlevel (e.g.,radioactive atom decay, collision of molecules in a gas) can produce predictable order with respect to at least certain macroscopic properties (e.g., half-life of radioactive decay, pressure-volume-temperature relations for a gas); *and* that systems that are deterministic and rule-obeying at one level can nevertheless exhibit a randomness, mathematical "chaos," at a higher level, so that they are unpredictable in the long run. Awareness of the existence of this latter—of the existence of chaotic dynamics in, particularly, dissipative systems—constitutes a major shift in our perception of the natural world ranging over the subject matter of many scientific disciplines, for example, ecology, meteorology, physics, chemistry, biochemistry, engineering, fluid mechanics, etc. Recognition of new fundamental limits to our ability to make predictions cannot but lead to a radical revision of the widely held presumption that we live in a predictable, because deterministic, world—an assumption othat has characterized much of our philosophizing (and indeed theologizing) hitherto.

Let me briefly—and it cannot but be inadequately both because of the time at my disposal and because I am not a mathematician—give you at least an impression of what these new developments are. They have in fact been a time-bomb ticking away under the edifice of the deterministic/predictable paradigm of what constitutes the worldview of science from at least as long ago as 1903. The French mathematician Henri Poincaré then pointed out that, since the ability of the (essentially Newtonian) theory of dynamical systems to make predictions depended on possessing knowledge concerning not only the "dynamic" (the rule(s) for describing how a system will change with time) but also knowledge of the initial conditions of the system, such predictability was extremely sensitive to the accuracy of our knowledge of the parameters characterizing those initial conditions.

Take, for example, the results of collisions between, say, billiard balls, occurring without loss of energy. An error on the thousandth decimal place in our knowledge of the angle of impact of the first collision has the consequence, as the errors accumulate and grow, that all knowledge of the velocities and positions of the individual balls would be lost after a thousand collisions. Or, more strikingly, suppose the colliding objects were gas molecules behaving in this respect like billiard balls. It turns out that the gravitational disturbance created by the movement of one electron at the edge of our galaxy would render the molecular motion unpredictable after only fifty collisions, that is, after about 10^{-10} seconds for such an assembly, or a minute for actual billiard balls. So, *pace* Laplace, detailed predictability is rapidly lost as the uncertainty increases with time. This lack of predictability has been obscured by the fact that it is usually not such detailed knowledge we are seeking. Thus, we do not want to know where each constituent unit has gone and how fast it is moving in the case of the assembly of gas molecules (though not, I would hasten to add, in the case of the billiards player!); all we want to know are macroscopic quantities such as the pressure, volume, and temperature, and these the kinetic theory of gases satisfactorily provides. But this relatively limited success has veiled the magnitude of our actual ignorance and inability to predict in this quite classical situation involving "closed" solutions.

This unpredictability arises from the increasing divergence of errors with time which entails a dependence on initial conditions that is so exquisitely sensitive that, for such systems, we know we can never acquire the accuracy desired for prediction, especially when eventually we have to enter the range of quantum uncertainty of variables. To put it another way, two very close, but not identical, initial states of such a system at first follow a course of development very close to each other but then increasingly diverge—and this happens however close we let the initial conditions be presumed to come. So even a committed classical Newtonian would have to admit that although, for example, we can calculate accurately enough for our purposes the trajectory through space of a ball or a spaceprobe, that of a flying balloon leaking air cannot be predicted. Mathematically, the answer is that although the dynamical relations of some systems can be expressed as differential equations that have "closed" solutions—that is, they will predict future states without going through all the intermediate ones—this is not true in general. For many natural systems, the controlling equations are nonlinear and one cannot predict the future from the initial conditions. Examples of such chaotic time dependence include turbulent flow in liquids; predator-prey patterns; stirred reactor systems that include autocatalytic relations; yearly variation in insect and other populations in nature; and the weather. The last-mentioned involves what has been called the "butterfly effect" (Edward Lorenz), whereby a butterfly disturbing the air here today could affect what weather occurs on the other side of the world in a month's time through the amplifications of errors and uncertainties cascading through a chain of complex interactions.

It is now realized that the time sequence of complex dynamical systems can take many forms. Those that have "closed" solutions to the relevant differential equations can settle down either to one particular state or oscillate, in a "limit cycle," between a sequence of states that are traversed periodically, like the pendulum of a grandfather clock. Or, consider chemical reaction systems. Normally, these are taken to come to the resting state of chemical equilibrium; but there are chemical systems, including some significant biochemical ones, that involve positive and negative feedback and, under particular initial conditions, settle down to regular oscillations in time and space with respect to the concentrations of key constituents. The same applies to populations of predators and prey. In both cases the mechanism involves particular values for the parameters that control formation/destruction of the units in question and their rate of movement through space. These are very striking phenomena to observe— startling even—and I mention them particularly because all this talk of "chaos" might obscure something that has, I think, been of particular significance for reflection on living systems—namely, the way *patterns* emerge in them.

What has transpired, as I read it, is that the mathematicians find that when they build up piecemeal, usually with the help of modern computers, the kind of solutions that are given by the nonlinear equations governing many natural complex dynamical systems, they find the following. Variation of a key controlling parameter (or parameters, in some cases) can at first lead to a single unique solution and all seems quite "normal" and well behaved from a determinist viewpoint—all is still predictable. (Their orbit in phase space exhibits a nonchaotic "attractor.") But at a certain critical value of this key parameter, the solutions bifurcate into two possible solutions, either of which may occur first as this critical point is passed, but *which* one is not predictable. As time proceeds, the system can "flip" between these two alternative allowed states and, under some circumstances, these interchanges can constitute regular oscillations. As the key parameter increases all kinds of further complexities can occur—further successive, numerous bifurcations into 4-states, 8-states, *ad infinitum*; periods of entirely erratic behavior, mathematically "chaotic"; and again bifurcations into 3-states, then 6-states, *etc.*. Finer and finer subdivisions numerically of the key parameters keep on repeating such sequences.

So the plots that mathematicians customarily use to depict changes in the state of a system (diagrams in "phase space") keep on revealing complexities and sequences of states at every level of magnification. In other words, they look like the pictures illustrating "fractals" with which Mandelbrot has familiarized us. Indeed, mathematically the regions in the phase space to which the systems gravitate (the states they tend to take up in ordinary language) can be proved to be fractals, having noninteger dimension and revealing more detail as they are progressively magnified. The line depicting the state of the system continuously folds back on itself going through states close to, but never identical with, previous ones—like dough, containing a drop of dye, that is kneaded by a baker. Such systems possess what is provokingly called a "strange attractor" to distinguish it from the more ordinary "attractors," the points, lines, or regions in phase space to which non-linear systems may move in time. This "fractal" character of the mathematical representation of these particular nonlinear systems is another way of expressing that special feature of their exquisite sensitivity to the values of their distinctive parameters which makes very close states in time lead to widely different results. In other words, small fluctuations in the system can lead to very large effects (the "butterfly effect" again) with loss of all predictive power.

In the real world most systems do not conserve energy: they are usually "dissipative" systems through which energy and matter flow, and so are also "open" in the thermodynamic sense. Such systems are typically characterized by the presence of "attractors" and they are often "strange attractors," giving rise to the kind of sequence just mentioned. At one set of values of a controlling system parameter there are nonchaotic attracting orbits, at first quite simple, representing an equilibrium or near-to-equilibrium or steady state in which typical characteristics of the system (e.g., reactant concentrations) do not vary with time. At somewhat higher values of this same system parameter, the solutions bifurcate and seemingly stable behavior occurs, patterned in space and/or time (e.g., limit cycles). This may be succeeded at still higher values of the controlling parameter by chaotic behavior. Many examples of this latter kind of system are now known: the formation of vertical hexagonal cells of convecting fluids in liquids heated from below; the transition to both irregular and periodic fluctuations in space and time of the concentrations of reactants in chemical systems that exhibit positive and negative feedback with diffusion; pattern formation in developing tissues through which both activators and inhibitors diffuse; the distribution of predators and prey in a particular territory; and so on.

Let us pause briefly to recognize how startling is this kind of behavior. To take the first example, one of the commonest in our experience: how is it that at a certain point in the heating of a liquid from below, all the molecules "decide" simultaneously to have a common upward component in their velocity and move upwards *together*? Or, how is it, in the famous Belousov-Zhabotinski reaction (see figure in chapter 1) that, at a given moment all the ceric and cerous ions at a particular physical level in a test tube "decide" simultaneously to be ceric, while in the band below they have all now become cerous ions and so alternately in horizontal bands down the tube? In both cases the system properties are causally effective in determining what happens to the components, even though the properties of the system itself depend on the individual properties of the components. An example of "top-down" causation, one would have to say or, rather, the co-presence of *both* "top-down" *and* "bottom-up" causation.

In the changeover to these temporal and spatial patterns of system behavior, we have examples of what Ilya Prigogine and his colleagues at Brussels have called "order through fluctuations."[7] For in these systems, at the critical points of bifurcation an arbitrary fluctuation has been amplified to such an extent that its scale becomes comparable in magnitude to that of the whole system and effectively takes it over, as it were, with a consequent transformation of the system's properties. A new regime emerges. In the last two decades, the Brussels school has studied the thermodynamics of such irreversible processes in open, dissipative systems that are a long way from equilibrium and are nonlinear (with respect to the relation between controlling fluxes and forces). Thermodynamics, one of the greatest scientific achievements of the last century and a half, comprises its famous second law to the effect that, in isolated systems undergoing natural irreversible processes, the entropy and "disorder" (appropriately defined) always increase. Ilya Prigogine and his colleagues were able to demonstrate that the emergence of new, more "ordered," or rather "organized," regimes were *required* by the thermodynamics for systems of this kind.

This work has special significance in relation to the quandary of our forbears in the nineteenth century who had to witness the apparent disjunction between, on the one hand, the second law prescribing increasing disorder, with the heat-death of equilibrium as the eventual outcome of all natural processes; and, on the other hand, their increasing conviction by Darwin that living organisms had evolved by a purely natural process, with emergence of increasingly complex and organized forms. The results of the Brussels school now show how living organisms might come into existence, swimming, as it were, against the entropic stream that carries all else to disorder. For living organisms are paradigm cases of open, nonlinear dissipative systems far from equilibrium and they depend for their existence on networks of chemical reactions (notoriously nonlinear in the required respect) which have positive and negative feedbacks and therefore are ripe to exhibit "order through fluctuations." The work of the Brussels school, together with that of Manfred Eigen and his colleagues at Göttingen[8] on the competitive kinetics of self-copying macromolecular systems, has succeeded in bridging the conceptual gulf which opened up in any consideration of the origin of life on the Earth—the gulf between nonliving and living matter. The entropic stream, we could say, flowing under constraints, generates patterned eddies near to its banks and these have included the protopatterns of living matter. We cannot go back and observe the first flicker of life in the primeval "soup" on the earth's surface. But we can now see from the work of Prigogine and Eigen et al. that the probability (Eigen says "inevitability") of its emergence is built in, as it were, into the kind of natural processes we actually have; and we can also see from the recent understanding of complex dynamical systems that such systems are fecund of new unexpected regimes and patterns—unpredictable beforehand, although intelligible *post hoc*.

Our reflections on "What's going on?" in the natural world, on "natural becoming," have given us a new awareness of the significance of time. Much of physics appeared to be time-reversible, which led to much heart searching when the second law appeared to give an arrow to time. The problems this generated concerning the relation of microscopic reversibility to macroscopic irreversibility have even now not been resolved to everyone's satisfaction. Macroscopic irreversible processes now transpire to be the necessary matrix for the emergence of new patterns and regimes in the natural world and the direction of their formation is that of increasing time (physicist's, clock time). Dissipative systems, with their particular dynamics, can generate new self-organizing, self-copying patterns in matter which then become irreversibly imprinted in the natural world so that a ratchet-like effect ensures their continuance. From the entropic stream there emerges dynamically the living with a new flexibility and open-endedness that the biologists have to learn to cope with. This, combined with our newly won awareness of the flexibility and unpredictability of complex physical systems with nonlinear dynamics, reinforces the judgment expressed in that striking description by the physicist Harold Schilling of time as the "locus of innovative change."

Our seeking of scientific answers to the questions about the world—"What's there?" and "What's going on?"—has opened up for us a new vista on the natural world, very different from that which prevailed in the mid-twentieth century. For we now have to recognize that the lawlike, deterministic dependabilities which the sciences unveil at some levels may so combine that they can, often unpredictably, lead to the emergence at other levels of systems of subtle complexities. In these systems, the behavior of the components depends not only on their well-established individual properties but also on the constraints exercized upon the parts by being incorporated into the whole—and some of these systems behave very surprisingly when viewed in the light only of the properties of the individual components. With respect to such systems, it is proper to speak, not only of the already recognized "bottom-up" type of causation whereby the properties of components affect those of the whole, but also of a "top-down" causative influence of the whole system on its components. For the system as a whole has emergent properties not obvious from those of the constituents and in many cases not strictly predictable from them. The irreducible concepts needed to describe the behavior of more complex systems, especially biological ones, frequently refer to and are aimed to depict—however provisionally, reviseably, and metaphorically— new realities that exist at those levels.

All these features acquire a new intensity and significance in living organisms. In biological evolution, the appearance of increasingly complex organisms and structures has become possible, along with the continued existence of many of the forms that precede them in the biological story. Myriad combinations of different kinds of skills and sensitivities are to be found appropriate to the biological niche of each living organism—and not least in the way individuality is combined with social organization. This complexity reaches its apogee in the human-brain-in-the-human-body which is the most complex organization of matter we know. The increasing flexibility and openendedness of natural processes is manifest in biological development as an increasing sensitivity to changes in the environment, based on complex anatomical and neurological elaboration. This is accompanied by a growth both in exploratory behavior and in the individuality of each organism as one follows the biological tree of evolution.

As nervous systems become more refined in their sensitivities, their information processing becomes more comprehensive and mobile creatures explore their environments. We then find it necessary to attribute a causative agency in their behavior for which we can only draw on analogies from our human experience—so we call it "consciousness," differing degrees of which we have to recognize in different creatures. In using such a word, we are not postulating the existence of any occult entity in the constitution of the higher mammals and primates. But we are recognizing that there is a "top-down" causative role that is played by some holistic state of the organisms, so that we cannot avoid using some such term to refer to aspects of their behavior which have parallels in our own. The understanding of the operation of the brains of the higher mammals and primates in terms of neuronal nets with the associated unpredictabilities that such nonlinear dynamic systems tend to display encourages one to think that here we might well have a physical corollary of those signs of decision making such organisms display. Successive states of the system as a whole are not strictly predictable from the states of individual components: the only available "logic" is the language we have available from our knowledge of the relationships we experience in the succession of our own mental states. These living creatures to which we tend to attribute consciousness manifest a significant development of that flexibility in response which is required for survival—in a world in which not only the crossing of unrelated causal chains can cause surprizes but also the unpredictabilities which we now recognize to be inherent even in their physical environment.

So far so good—but there is an Achilles heel to the whole exposition up to this point. For we have failed to include a singular actualization of the potentialities inherent in the natural processes of the world—namely, *ourselves*. We have failed to ask that further question about the natural order, "*Who*'s there?" The most striking feature of the universe is one so obvious that we often overlook it—the fact that we are here to ask questions about it at all! That the regular laws of nature acting upon and in the entities and through the processes we have been considering should, in the course of time, have culminated in an entity, humanity, which can know the route by which it has arrived on the scene, is an astonishing outcome of that highly condensed nodule of matter-energy enfolded in the tight knot of space-time with which this universe began. Attempts to delineate what constitutes the *humanum*, the distinctively human, are legion and any account attempted by me at this late stage of this paper could only be painfully inadequate. The evolutionary biologist Konrad Lorenz, concerned with evolutionary epistemology, lists[9] as "integrated into systems of a higher order" a number of cognitive functions also to be found in animals, namely: the perception of form which then constitutes a mechanism of both abstraction and objectivization; the central representation of space, especially through sight; locomotion, following on from visual orientation; memory, storing of information, as the learned basis of insight-controlled behavior; voluntary movement in conjunction with the feedback it produces; exploratory behavior; imitation, the basis for the learning of verbal languages; and tradition, the transmission of individually acquired knowledge from one generaton to another. Human beings have a capacity for self-awareness—we use the word "I" of ourselves in semantically peculiar ways—which is the root both of our capacity for intersubjective communication and the integrating activity which gives each of us our sense of personhood, of being a particular *person*. As Ian Ramsey put it:

> personality [is] to be analysed in terms of a distinctive activity, distinctive in being owned, localized, personalized. The unity of the personality...is to be found in an integrating activity, an activity expressed, embodied and scientifically

understood in terms of its genetic, biochemical, [etc.]...man-
ifestations. What we call human behaviour is an expression
of that effective, integrating activity which is peculiarly and
distinctively ourselves.[10]

This "integrating activity" includes our sense of being agents in
the world, making choices for what appear to be "reasons"—even
though these are often the net sum of complex motivations other than
the rational. In such decisions we have the experience of free choice
and of not being deterministic systems controlled by the laws that the
natural sciences have hitherto supposed to tell us determine pre-
dictably all that goes on in the natural world.

We have been surveying what science is today telling us broadly
about the world. It now appears that the world contains entities in a
hierarchy of complexity in which complex systems manifest genuinely new realities and that these emerge in time by processes which,
although resting on deterministic laws at one level, nevertheless can
unpredictably produce intricate sequences of events and new entities.
Among these, the emergence of human personhood must be reckoned
as both the most unpredictable *ante hoc* and the most significant. The
integrating activity that constitutes our personhood, both at the individual level of the sense of being an "I" and at the intersubjective
level of human society and culture, is distinctive and genuinely emergent. Yet it arises out of an order of natural being and becoming that
contains features the extrapolation and development of which make
this emergence possible.

The cosmological anthropic principle has already in our generation served to demonstrate, whatever other conclusions might be
drawn from it, that the existence of all life, including human, is
closely bound up with this universe having particular values of certain, basic physical parameters that control its physical form. Were
they to be even minutely different, life, and we, would not have been
possible. Now, I am suggesting, our *scientific* perspective no longer,
if indeed it ever did, precludes, or makes absurd, or reduces to nullity,
both the naturalness *and* distinctiveness of human personhood, freedom, and consciousness. These can be recovered as genuine realities
in the world—part of the data awaiting conceptual explication based
on experience (and experiments, a scientist would say). For the natural world itself, in its being and becoming, has inbuilt propensities to:
complexity; open-endedness; flexibility; and "top-down" causation
from higher systemic levels of complexity to lower, as well as the reverse. This renders coherent and plausible the possibility of there
emerging a self-consciousness as the holistic self-referring state of a

brain-in-a-body that could be a free, self-aware, thinking being—in fact, a person. As Crutchfield et al. conclude:

> Even the process of intellectual progress relies on the injection of new ideas and on new ways of connecting old ideas. Innate creativity may have an underlying chaotic process that selectively amplifies small fluctuations and molds them into macroscopic coherent mental states that are experienced as thoughts. In some cases the thoughts may be decisions, or what are perceived to be the exercise of will. In this light, chaos provides a mechanism that allows for free will within a world governed by deterministic laws.[11]

It is now becoming at least intelligible, *post hoc*, as with all genuine emergents, how natural being and becoming could be the matrix of the personal—the chrysalis of the human. *That* humanity is itself now faced with the awesome recognition that it could be the "butterfly" the cumulative effects of whose unconsidered actions might be amplified, precipitating consequences for nature, its chrysalis, of an unimaginably catastrophic *or* fulfilling magnitude.

Some chrysalis—some butterfly!

But now a further question presses itself on us as we reflect on this natural world that includes ourselves. There are propensities that are manifest in the processes of natural becoming that reach their fullest expression in ourselves—the dice appear to be loaded in our direction. *Why* are the dice so loaded? Any answer to such a question of such cosmic import, any inference to the best explanation at *this* level, can resort only to concepts that aim to depict a reality which is causative in a "top-down" modality on the total complex of the world system; and operates at a level analogous to, and an extrapolation of, that most complex, open, dissipative, free, flexible level that we know—that of *human* agency.

So, appropriately two hundred years after the establishment of Georgetown University with its distinctive ethos, the Enlightenment has run its course and our contemporary scientific perspective presses on our culture an old question in a new form:

Who loaded the dice?

REFERENCES

1.   John Donne, "An Anatomie of the World: The First Anniversary," in C. A. Plerides, ed., *The Complete English Poems of John Donne* (London: Dent, 1985).

2. Herbert Butterfield, *The Origins of Modern Science 1300-1800* (London: Bell, 1968 edition), vii.

3. Jarrett Leplin, *Scientific Realism* (Berkeley and London: University of California Press, 1984), 2.

4. Ernan McMullin, "A Case for Scientific Realism," in Jarrett Leplin, op. cit., 26.

5. Francis H. C. Crick, *Of Molecules and Man* (Seattle: University of Washington Press, 1966), 10.

6. James P. Crutchfield, J. Doyne Farmer, Norman H. Packard and Robert S. Shaw, "Chaos," *Scientific American* (December 1986), 38.

7. Q.v., *inter alia*, Ilya Prigogine, *From Being to Becoming* (San Francisco: Freeman, 1980); Ilya Prigogine and Isabelle Stengers, *Order Out of Chaos* (London: Heinemann, 1984); and the exposition of these ideas given in Arthur R. Peacocke, *An Introduction to the Physical Chemistry of Biological Organization* (Oxford: Clarendon Press, 1983), chap. 2.

8. Manfried Eigen and Peter Schuster, *The Hypercycle* (Berlin: .Springer-Verlag, 1979); Manfried Eigen and Ruthild Winkler, *Laws of the Game* (New York and London: Knopf and Allen Lane, 1982); also expounded in Peacocke, op.cit., chap. 7.

9. Konrad Lorenz, *Behind the Mirror* (English trans., London: Methuen, 1977) chap. 7, 113 ff.

10. Ian T. Ramsey, "Human Personality," in *Personality and Science: An Interdisciplinary Discussion*, I. T. Ramsey and R. Porter, eds. (Edinburgh and London: Churchill Livingstone, 1971), 128.

11. Op. cit., 49.

5 : 2

THE PHILOSOPHICAL PROBLEM
OF INDIVIDUALS IN PHYSICS

Ivor Leclerc

The problem of individuals in physics is also, as I shall endeavor to show, a philosophical problem, one which has profound implications for science. In the modern period the conception of individuals in physics is that which had been authoritatively accepted by Newton in the seventeenth century. He stated this as follows:

> All these things being consider'd, it seems probable to me, that God in the Beginning form'd Matter in solid, massy, hard, impenetrable, movable Particles, of such Sizes and Figures, and with such other Properties, and in such Proportion to Space, as most conduced to the End for which he form'd them; and that these primitive Particles being Solids, are incomparably harder than any porous Bodies compounded of them; even so very hard, as never to wear or break in pieces; no ordinary Power being able to divide what God himself made one in the first Creation.[1]

This is the theory of material atomism, that is, the conception of the ultimate physical individual as an atomic (i.e., not further divisible) particle of matter, a "body" *per se*. This conception was accepted in the succeeding centuries, and is that which continues, as a tacit presupposition, to influence present-day thought.

Now it is highly important to recognize that Newton's theory had, at the time, constituted the introduction of an entirely new conception of matter, displacing a conception of matter which had derived from Aristotle, and which had been accepted through the Middle Ages and the Renaissance. In this antecedent conception, matter was a substrate which underlay the forms of definiteness. It was not itself any kind of physical being or existent, as it became in the Newtonian system. Instead, matter as a substrate had been conceived as a principle[2] or source of physical entities, for in this older conception matter had been the recipient of forms; and it was by virtue of this that physical bodies came into being. But in Newton's theory the conception of a substrate was entirely abandoned, and the physical existent, the physical body, was held to be matter *per se.*

Because of the success of Newton's physics his theory of the material, the physical, individual came fairly quickly into general acceptance—displacing the rival theories of Descartes and Leibniz, for example. Further, in the course of the next two centuries, this theory of matter *per se* as the physical existent had become so fully accepted that it acquired the status of a self-evident presupposition, accepted without question.

That this was so is exemplified at the end of the nineteenth century when it was discovered that what had been identified as atoms were in fact not "atomic," i.e., indivisible, but that they were composite. It was not, however, recognized that this discovery constituted the destruction of the theory of material atomism, and physicists proceeded conceiving the subatomic constituents as material particles-this being indeed signified by the use of the word "particle," meaning a small part, of matter.

This presupposition, however, is shown by their own work to be definitely unwarrantable, for these subatomic entities, it has transpired, are quite evidently of different *kinds*—and, as Newton was quite clear, "matter," in his theory, does not admit of differences of kind, or of quality, but only of quantity.

One further implication of this Newtonian theory was of major import. This is that Newton, by rejecting matter, not only as a substrate, but also as a principle or source, had deprived the physical itself of any inherent source of motion. In the Newtonian conception, material particles are wholly inert, devoid of any power of change or motion; as Newton said in the passage quoted earlier, they are "movable," but do not in any respect move themselves. Newton's answer to this problem was to have recourse to a wholly transcendent source of motion. In his theory God was required to move matter.

In contrast to this, in Aristotle's theory the principle or source of motion and change was not transcendent, but inherent in nature, in the physical. Aristotle regarded matter not only as the recipient of forms, but also as the principle of motion of the physical, and hence characterized matter as *dunamis*, power, potency, potentiality.

Now it seems clear that in twentieth-century physics, in contrast to the antecedent Newtonian physics, the various subatomic "particles" are far from being "inert." They are not merely passively subject to locomotion, change of place. On the contrary, it is evident that they are "active," that "energy" is attributed to them—that is, they have the capacity to do work, to effect changes, and to affect others.

I want to urge that in the present juncture of thought it is of the greatest moment to recur to the crucially important distinction which Aristotle recognized between, on the one hand, the physical existents themselves, and on the other, the principles or sources, which are immanent in nature. In this century one thinker, A. N. Whitehead, did come to a recognition of that distinction between the actual physical entities and the substrate principle from which they derive—although he did not get very far in working out its implications for contemporary physics.[3] But he did maintain, what is most important, that this substrate—which he called creativity—must be the source, the principle, of activity in the physical, and it seems to me that this must be accepted. However, this does not mean that the substrate is some kind of active "thing" or existent; it is a "principle," i.e., source of activity in existent things.

The substrate must be conceived as *dunamis*—a power, potency, potentiality—which is "actualized" in individual "acts" or "actings." Each act occurs and, *as* that act, is over, past. It then has to be superseded by another act; and so on, continuously. Here we have, at the philosophical level, the quantization which is now so familiar in contemporary physics. What we have here is in fact the philosophical basis of the quantum in physics.

But each act is not *per se* what would be considered a physical individual. Such an individual must be identifiable, and what occurs simply once hardly qualifies for identity. A physical individual must be constituted by at least a route of supersession of actings. Necessitated too is a particular "definiteness," which is identical, the same, throughout the route of actings, and which makes the particular individual identifiable as such.

A further, quite fundamental, feature of acting needs to be recognized. This is that acting is necessarily relational: as both Plato and Aristotle were very clear, acting entails an "acting on" (*poiein*) and a "being acted on" (*paschein*). This is the very contrary of a Newtonian material individual, which stands in no relation at all to any other—this is what is meant by saying that the relations of the material individual are entirely "external."

Thus in terms of the philosophical theory being adumbrated here, the individual actings in a route of supersession are sequentially related. This sequential relating constitutes the philosophical basis of *time* or temporal order in the physical realm. A route of actings in supersession can also involve change of position in relation to other actings; *this* relational acting constitutes the philosophical basis of spatial order in the physical realm. Thus both temporal and spatial order are philosophically grounded in the substrate *dunamis*. This is to be seen in contrast to Newton's doctrine, in which space and time each had a separate, and unexplained, status as some kind of absolute—they are simply introduced, but not explained, in the first Scholium in his *Principia*.[4]

Newton also introduced the concept of "force" in his "Axioms, or Laws of Motion," in that context the force being "motive force." Again here "force" is assumed, without any explanation. In the theory I am advocating, "force" is also philosophically grounded in the substrate *dunamis*, power, potency. In this century physics has come to recognize a multiplicity of forces, and in this, one feature has become prominent, namely, that the various kinds of force—gravitational, electromagnetic, strong, weak, etc.,—all involve relationships, indeed, do not exist except in relationships.

This means, from the philosophical point of view, that what is recognized as "force" is the product of "relational acting." For acting *is* relational; it entails "being acting on," and "reacting to." Thus, acting involves polarity: the positive-negative contrast. This contrast is necessary for the perpetuation of any particular definiteness which provides the identity of the individual—it is other than, and elsewhere, and elsewhen, any other. Consequently, all contrast involves difference, and thus different possibilities—possibility for actualization. It thus becomes intelligible how contrasting polarity can constitute what is now distinguished in physics as "binding force" or "strong force," for this is necessary for the maintenance and perpetuation of the definiteness, the identity, of any physical actuality. Herein lies the philosophical explanation for structured unity in the notion of, for example, an atom and its constituents—of why it has to be the way it is.

In conclusion, I shall elaborate specifically on the notion of the physical individual. The conception of the physical individual, the existent, as essentially and fundamentally matter, as a corporeal, a bodily entity, persists in this century despite the discovery of the quantum by Planck and Einstein. This is due to this discovery having been connected with energy, which seemed somehow distinct from matter. Thus each subatomic particle continues on the whole to be assumed to be one singular existent throughout a spatio-temporal passage from one location to another. Therefore, not only its existence, but also its individuality and identity, continue implicitly to be conceived of as grounded in the Newtonian theory of matter.

But if the theory of matter be rejected—as we have seen it must be—then existence and individuality must be grounded in acting. But the identity cannot be grounded in the acting *qua* act; it can only be grounded in the definiteness, the character, of the acting, for it is definiteness alone which is repeatable, and can be *idem*, the same.

Thus there is an identity achieved through a succession of superseding acts, and it is such a route of succession which constitutes an individual, i.e., a physical existent.

However, as we have seen, by reason of the essential interrelatedness of all acting, these individuals, depending upon their definitenesses, will be relationally closely associated with other individuals, thus constituting a unity—for example, an "atomic" unity of protons, electrons, etc. Such a compound can be treated as an individual, since it preserves its identity through spatio-temporal changes.

For the most part present-day science, as I have already said, continues to operate on the tacit presupposition of these "physical existents," or "individuals," being "matter" in the Newtonian sense of indivisible "stuff," resulting in a continuation of the conception of the universe as a mechanism, prevalent since Descartes and Galileo in the seventeenth century and perfected by Newton. Because in that view the physical was conceived as matter, the word "matter" is also today frequently used by scientists, by philosophers, by laymen, in the general sense of "that which physically exists." Further, although matter has been shorn, by work in modern physics as well as by revolutionary work in other branches of science, of the entire Newtonian connotation, it continues through its common usage to perpetuate presuppositions no longer applicable or valid.

The problem of the "individual" has become acute in our time. Is the individual adequately conceived as "that which preserves its self-identity through spatio-temporal changes"? The issue is what precisely this "self-identity" consists in. In the Newtonian conception it consisted in its being the self-same piece or particle of matter which was in place A, and now is in place B. But the twentieth-century developments have made this conception untenable. For if, as I have argued above, it has become necessary in the present-day context to recognize that the factor of "acting" is fundamental, then the analysis of "self-identity" becomes much more complex. For while in the transition of the entity from place A to place B there is a self-identity of the "definiteness" or "character" of the entity, there can be no identity of "act." There is one acting at spatio-temporal location A, but since a single act is over and done, it must be a numerically other act which occurs at spatio-temporal location B.

Now one most important significance of this is that the act at location B is not absolutely determined to re-enact the definiteness of the antecedent act at location A. It could also, and in addition, respond to other neighboring antecedent acts, its character thus being affected by its integral ambient conditions. It is these conditions which will determine, for example, whether at B there occurs a transmission of an electronic, protonic, or other character or a burst of radiation. My main point is that the nature, kind and character of a subatomic entity is much more readily intelligible in terms of relational acting than it can be in the conception of self-identical entities simply in transition from one place to another. For it is manifest that spatio-temporal transition cannot have a simple ultimacy so often supposed in the Newtonian theory—incorrectly so, since even in that theory it had to be dependent upon God's act.

There is one further point very pertinent to the problem of the physical individual. This is with respect to the concept of "force," which has come to be so crucially important in the last half-century in research into the subatomic "particles." Newton had insisted that natural science, and mechanics in particular, is concerned with force (specifically gravitational) only in respect of "quantities and mathematical properties"; he particularly eschewed "all questions about the nature or quality of this force."[5] Newton had been followed in this course by Laplace in the eighteenth century, and by the most significant natural scientists in the nineteenth century and on into the twentieth. In the last half-century, however, the issue of the *nature* of "force" has willy-nilly obtruded especially upon scientists working in the area of elementary particles. In addition to gravitational force, three others, of different *kinds*, have been distinguished, namely, electromagnetic, weak, and strong forces. It is to be noted that this evidently entails implicitly introducing considerations of "nature" and "quality." Further, it is significant that all these forces have also come to be thought of as constituting "interactions"—gravitational, electromagnetic, weak and strong interactions. Now it is to be observed that this implies "agency" and "agents," which is inconsistent with the persisting view of the elementary particles conceived on the model of material bodies in motion. This conception entailed an ontological duality of force and matter which, however, is no longer tenable in the light of contemporary findings in research on what is still, on the basis of that model, termed elementary "particles." A quite different view of the physical is evidently requisite, one which, as I have proposed, conceives the physical in terms of "acting." On the basis of this, instead of the earlier duality, forces can be consistently understood in terms of the quantum relational acting of the physical existents.

REFERENCES

1.   Issac Newton, *Opticks* (New York: Dover Publications, Inc.; London: Constable & Co., 1952), 400.

2.   It is important to note that the word "principle" here, and throughout this paper, is that given in the O.E.D., art. I: "Origin, source; source of action. 2. That from which something takes its rise, originates, or is derived; a source." It is *not* the meaning given in art. II: "Fundamental truth, law, or motive force. 5. A fundamental truth or proposition, on which many others depend; a primary truth comprehending, or forming the basis of, various subordinate truths." The latter sense is that most commonly occurring in modern natural science.

3.   See Alfred N. Whitehead, *An Equiry Concerning the Principles of Natural Knowledge* (Cambridge: Cambridge University Press, 1919), in which the concept of "events" was introduced; *Science and the Modern World* (New York: Macmillan, 1925); a paper on "Time," in *Proc. Sixth International Congress of Philosophy*, 1926 (held at Harvard University).

4.   Issac Newton, *Mathematical Principles of Natural Philosophy*, F. Cajori, ed. (Berkeley: University of California, 1962), vol. 2, 6.

5.   Newton, op.cit., vol. 2, 550.

6 : 1

THE ROLE OF MORALS AND INCENTIVES IN SOCIETY

Mancur Olson

I

A society, if it's going to work well, requires not only widespread adherence to appropriate moral codes, but also an appropriate structure of incentives. A good structure of incentives gives the individuals in a society a reason, given individual self-interest, to behave in ways that improve the performance of that society and the quality of life in it. In other words, I think of morals and incentives not as opposites or enemies but rather as indispensable partners, both of which are needed if we are to have a well-functioning society. We also need the right division of labor between the partners: we must note the circumstances in which reliance on morals, on the one hand, or incentives, on the other, will be most suitable.

The problem of morals and incentives in societies begins, in a way, with the fact that *morality is a scarce resource*. I have never heard anyone complain that the human race has too much morality, but many complain that it has too little. Even after millennia of preaching, morality is still in short supply. There have been lots of good preachers over the last few thousand years, and yet in no society has moral and altruistic behavior been so plentiful that it alone has been sufficient to make a society thrive.

I am not suggesting that moral behavior is rare or characteristic of only a few saintly types. Some amount of moral behavior seems to me to be general in every society that I know anything about. Since there are some people, especially in my discipline of economics, who regard altruism as aberrational or nonexistent, we must show them

that there is *indisputable* evidence of general altruism. We can see
that there is such indisputable evidence in a prosaic observation that
all of us have made. Suppose you are lost (in any neighborhood, rich
or poor, in any city or any country). If you ask for directions, in the
overwhelming preponderance of cases, you get them, and you get
them for free. Now that's a banal observation, but it nonetheless tells
you that the willingness to help others (some degree of altruism) is
virtually universal. Similarly, when there is an accident—when someone is bleeding profusely or there is a heart attack—people nearby
will almost always help. There are a few well-known cases where this
has not happened, but I suspect that in these cases many individuals
assumed that others are in fact dealing with the problem. So I treat
moral impulses as general characteristics of the population, not as
something that is exceptional.

Yet these impulses, though nearly universal, are by themselves
nonetheless not sufficient, *not* strong enough nor regular enough, to
make a society work. When it comes to getting society's hard work
done on a day-in-day-out basis—when it comes to getting lots of irk-
some and distasteful effort out of a population regularly over many
years—it generally appears that morals alone are not enough. The experience of many communes, many countries, and many inadequately
funded charities supports the observation that morals alone are not
enough.

There are also corroborating observations from the experiences
of nations at times when there is national consensus about the urgency
of some national need. Suppose we take nations during wars, especially wars where there is a consensus in the population that the nation
is right and that it ought to win the war. Even in these circumstances,
altruistic impulses are not sufficient to finance the war effort. Every
country in these circumstances needs taxes or compulsory payments in
order to finance its war effort. There have never been any exceptions
to this rule for any large society. This is a general instance of the theory of public goods and the logic of collective action.[1]

Thus there can be no doubt that societies need to use incentives,
especially in those circumstances where the moral impulse is not even
close to being sufficient. One well-known way in which incentives are
used to get the world's work done is, of course, through competitive
markets. The proposition that there are many circumstances in which
competitive markets can lead self-interested people to behave in ways
that generate a desirable social outcome goes back all the way to
Adam Smith. This argument about markets is so well known and so
familiar that I don't think it is necessary to dwell on it for long.
Almost everyone realizes that in certain circumstances markets can

function effectively for a society. We all know that there are a variety of market economies, like our own, with reasonable economic performance, and now everyone knows of the economic failures of Soviet-type societies. Thus the idea that the market can harness the self-interest of people to generate desirable social outcomes is one of which most educated people are already aware. There are all sorts of interesting questions about the circumstances in which markets will work well and the circumstances in which they will not, and some of my research focuses on these questions. There is by now a precise and subtle theory of markets that largely explains when there will be market success and when there will be market failure, but since this theory is one that many people already know, I will not repeat it here.

II

I would like instead to focus on the role of incentives, not in markets in any narrow sense of the word, but on the role of incentives in government and politics, and even on the role of incentives in the emergence of government and the creation of the institutional environment that makes markets possible. In other words I'd like to look at an area where I claim, by and large, people have neglected the role of incentives, but where incentives are nonetheless very important.

One line of thinking, going back to the great French sociologist Emile Durkheim, and developed by the American sociologist Talcott Parsons and others, argues that markets will only exist if three is a *prior* moral order.[2] It is said that there are "non-contractual elements in contracts" and that contracts rest on a moral order that precedes the market. In this view, a common religion (or something of that sort) is necessary if markets are to function well. So, one line of reasoning looks to the development of moral codes (perhaps through religions) for the prerequisites for the market. The moral codes include beliefs that contracts should be honored, that the property of other people should be respected, and so on, and these beliefs make markets work in a satisfactory way.

I'm sure that there is something in this line of thinking, but it is overdrawn. We can see how it is overdrawn, and get some ideas on how to make our own society and government work better, if we look at the emergence of law and order and government. Governments also are important in explaining the enforcement of contracts and of property rights.

Let's ask ourselves, "How do law and order and government emerge?" If you go back far enough in human history, mankind was in tiny hunter-gatherer bands made up mostly of blood relatives. This was the phase of history that Marx called "primitive communism". The anthropologists tell us that the hunter-gatherer band is a very small unit and that it is usually governed by consensus—by voluntary cooperation of the few families involved.

It turns out, when one examines the logic of collective action closely, that small groups—groups that have fewer than ten families, as the typical primitive hunter-gatherer band did—can often cooperate spontaneously and provide themselves with what economists call "public goods" voluntarily. So I do not want here to look in detail at hunter-gatherer bands and their elementary systems of order, which are more or less on an extended family scale.

III

I would like instead to ask: "How does a peaceful order emerge when there are thousands or millions of people? How does government emerge in an environment with thousands or millions of people if there is initial anarchy?" My thinking about these questions developed when, by chance, I was reading the biography of a Chinese warlord.[3] From about World War I up to the early thirties, much of China was under the control of warlords. A leader of a band of armed men (some "entrepreneur" specializing in the use of force) would conquer a particular province or locality, and then take advantage of his conquest by taxing the people and appointing himself the lord or governor of the area. There was no central government with control over the whole of the country. Now in reading about one of these warlords named Feng, I noticed that there was a struggle between this warlord's army and a similar-sized army of a roving bandit, whose name translated as "White Wolf". White Wolf's army was much feared and thought to be a match for the warlord's army. There was a battle between the warlord's army and White Wolf's army. The warlord's army, it turned out, won and the roving bandit's army was defeated. Feng became famous for putting down bandits and became popular: his subjects were sorry to lose him. According to the book I was reading, the people were joyous that the warlord's army was used to repress bandits and that the roving bandit armies were defeated.

IV

When I read that I thought, "how arbitrary!" What legitimacy does a warlord have? A warlord is nothing but a *stationary* bandit, and thus morally no better than a *roving* bandit. By what moral principle do we prefer a warlord, who just happens to do his banditry on a fixed location with taxes rather than by roving around? But later, I got to thinking that perhaps the people who were joyous about the warlord's victory over the roving bandit army were right, and that I was wrong.

Suppose we ask what the situation of ordinary people would be when there are just roving bandits, as compared with the situation of the people when there are stationary warlords who defeat the roving bandits and engage in tax-theft instead. The roving bandit takes what he finds and moves on. But the stationary warlord has an incentive to get as much tax revenue as he possibly can. But how can he get the most tax revenue?

He will get the maximum in tax theft only if the domain that he has conquered is productive. The more income that is generated in his domain, the more he can collect in taxes. A good stationary bandit, a good warlord, will make sure that there are incentives to produce; he will, in other words, provide law and order (including law and order with respect to tradeables, which we call "property rights"). With law and order there will be a great increase in production. People will believe, if they expect law and order to continue, that if they produce something they will be able to keep that part of it which does not go into tax revenue. They will, moreover, have incentives to invest, because law and order will mean that they will be able to keep the goods and machines that they have invested in. The stationary bandit or warlord has an incentive not to allow *anyone else* to steal because that will mean less for him, so apart from his taxes there is no other theft allowed.

In short, a bandit will maximize his receipts from thievery if he settles down and establishes himself as a lord or as a king who provides law and order and other public goods, and takes all his theft in the form of predictable taxes. By contrast, if his armed force instead is used for roving banditry, then there will be very little production. People will only produce things that they can hide or consume promptly. There will be a very low level of output indeed, and this will even generate problems for the roving bandits. In anarchy there is not much for roving bandits to steal.

I am suggesting that, in some sense, the beginning of ancient or classical civilization was probably, in many cases, the result of the incentive that conquerors had to set themselves up in the business of government, because what they could get in theft through tax collection was greater than what they could get by migratory pillage. Law and order, then, was something there was sometimes an *incentive* for a conqueror to provide. *The first blessing of the invisible hand was government*! The invisible hand led the conqueror to provide law and order and other public goods because this made his take larger.

V

I got to thinking of this matter from another angle when I was reading Edward Banfield's *The Moral Basis of a Backward Society.*[4] In a village in one of the poor parts of southern Italy, Banfield was talking to the local people and getting the local *mores*. He happened to talk to the village monarchist. The village monarchist was a believer, not in constitutional monarchy or limited monarchy, but in old-fashioned absolute monarchy. I thought "how quaint and strange." Perhaps the best way to sum up the monarchist's case is in questions and answers. The monarchist asks, "If you owned a house and the roof leaked you'd fix it, wouldn't you?" The answer is, "Yes, of course." "Aha says the monarchist, "if Italy has a king and something is broke, the king will have an incentive to fix it because the king owns the country!"

When I first read the monarchist's argument, it outraged my democratic sensibilities. But I also couldn't put the monarchist's argument out of my mind, because obviously there was a germ of truth in it. A king does indeed have an incentive to make sure that his domain is productive and in good repair. Indeed, the insight of this Italian monarchist, whose argument troubled me so, is really the insight that I'm arguing applies also to the people who preferred that the warlord-bandit win out over the roving bandit. There is an incentive for the bandit who settles down (or for the king, pharaoh, or emperor) to provide law and order and other public goods. The reason is that, if their power is secure, they own the country or the domain, just as we own our houses. If the property is well taken care of and provided with public goods such as law and order, there are higher tax receipts for the king (or pharaoh or emperor or warlord) who owns the domain.

Given my own democratic sensibilities, the foregoing argument is troubling. It suggests that maybe dictatorship is not so terribly bad—that maybe we should condone the old-fashioned monarchies and autocratic empires of predemocratic times, and the dictators of undemocratic parts of the world today. As a convinced democrat, I have been troubled for a long while by the idea that there is in dictatorship, in warlordship, and in kingship, an incentive to make societies work. So I have had to ask myself the question, "Is it possible that, contrary to what I have always believed, dictatorship is better than democracy, because the dictator will have an incentive to make the society work?" This is not, for me at least, a comfortable question.

Section VI

Interestingly, thinking about this question tells us something about reforms that could possibly improve the working of our own democracy. It is true that the stationary bandit or king will have an incentive to make his domain productive. But the same self-interest that converts him from roving bandit to government means that he wants the *maximum possible tax revenues*. This is not so appealing.

Admittedly, the warlord or king will have an incentive to maximize tax *collections*, not tax *rates*. Hundred percent taxes would collect nothing in revenue. But the tax rate, or the level or feudal dues and exactions, that maximizes the total take of the king is the one that the king or pharaoh has an incentive to impose. There is a lot of evidence that many dictators, kings, and pharaohs have really tried to maximize their tax collections. Whether you look at the old regime in France before the French Revolution, or at the dictatorial periods of the Roman Empire, or at some dictatorships today, you find, in a great number of cases, that the dictators are trying to take the maximum amount they can in tax collections. To be sure, even if the king lives in unimaginable splendor—even if he builds himself palaces like Versailles—that will take only a small percentage of the national income of a country as big as France, for example. But one of the things that we observe is that kings and warlords use a large part of their revenue for wars for their personal aggrandizement. Kings maximize their tax collections for the purpose of war as well as for palaces.

In other words, one part of an autocratic ruler's consumption is in the form of competition with other warlords and kings. They will try to outdo their competitors, the other warlords and kings, by getting a bigger domain, if possible a huge empire. This is an understandable motive for a conqueror, but it is still very expensive for the people who have to pay taxes and feudal dues and also sometimes die in the wars that are part of the dictator's consumption pattern. So we can see that, even though the king is trying to make the society work, he is trying to make it work so that he can milk the maximum amount out of it. Needless to say, that is not the sort of thing that is best for the subjects. It's better than being a victim or roving bandits, but it is hardly the best sort of situation.

Section VII

Now let's try to construct the simplest intellectual device or model we can usefully employ to examine a pertinent aspect of democracy. The little democratic model I'm going to put forth is so simple that it doesn't adequately describe any country, but that's not the purpose of it. The purpose is to get the simplest possible way to understand a previously unrecognized incentive in many democratic societies. This is a wholesome incentive we can make stronger in real-world democracies and thereby make them work better.

Suppose that we have a two-party democracy. In order to simplify things, let's not think of political parties as they are in our country, where they are somewhat undisciplined and fragmented. (As we know, an individual congressman or an individual senator will often maximize his or her chances for reelection by trying to get favors for the district—"pork" for the district—or by trying to do the work of special-interest lobbies and so getting campaign contributions from them, rather than by being loyal to his party.) Much of what goes on in the U.S. political system is not explained by political parties. That is not the fault of the Democrats, or of the Republicans; it is a result of the fact that there are limits to the power of each of these parties.

So let's now think of what incentive a party that was really disciplined and clearly in charge would face. We can see what this incentive is, more or less, by looking at the incentives facing our presidents. While it is true that presidents may not control the Congress, nonetheless they know that (if they run for reelection) they will face one major opponent in the general election. So the United States has two-person, two-party competition at least in presidential elections. Thus, in some degree, we can think of the presidential elections as prototypical, or as embodying the type of two-party competition that I will focus on.

If a political party in a two-party democracy wants to get reelected, then what kind of public policies will it have an incentive to adopt? Will its incentive be like the dictator's incentive to maximize tax collections? Surely not. The best way to get reelected is to persuade at least a majority of the electorate that their welfare will be higher if they reelect the existing party than if they replace it with the opposition.

The welfare of the electorate depends on the *net* benefit of the government's actions for the citizenry. If a party succeeds in making the country work well, and succeeds in making it work in the interest of the electorate (or at least the majority of the electorate), then it will have a better chance of getting reelected by this electorate. Thus the party will, of course, collect taxes, but it has an incentive to use this taxation to provide public goods and transfers to the citizenry. The average voter is not very well informed and there is a lot of misrepresentation. Still, when other things are equal, a party or president will have the best opportunities for reelection if the party or the president has that level of taxes and that type of public expenditure that best serve the interests of the citizenry.

As observation reveals, an incumbent party (or president) has a better chance of reelection if there is peace and prosperity, so it has an incentive to choose policies that generate peace and prosperity. Now I am not suggesting that any democracy I know (including the one headquartered in Washington) works in the idealized or simple way that I have just described. One of the things that I've devoted a lot of my working life to is writing about the depredations of distributional coalitions or special-interest groups.[5] One of the things that happens in our democracy is that organized groups find it in their interest to lobby or to collude and cartelize in ways which are good for them but bad for the country. So I'm not saying the simple model that I just described does justice to the current American scene, or for that matter to any other country.

But the simple model does, nonetheless, tell us something. And that is, that when we introduce democratic procedures there are officials or parties that can be held responsible for how well the society is working—for *outcomes*. When democratic institutions are structured so that it is clear who is in charge, then those who are in charge can be held responsible and the outcomes for the country can be attributed, in part, to the government or misgovernment of the official or party in charge. When we have that situation, we have a party or official with an incentive to behave in such a way that the welfare of the citizenry—or at least a majority of the citizenry—is taken into account.

Note that in this sort of situation you will not get the maximum level of tax collections. It can be proven that when tax collections are at a maximum the interests of citizens are *not* maximized. A party in a two-party system will not have the incentive a dictator has to maximize tax collections.

Section VIII

I am, accordingly, suggesting that even in the realm of government (not only in the market place) it pays to think about how to improve the structure of incentives. A well-working democracy, in my opinion, is one where the incentives faced by politicians are incentives consistent with good government—government in the interest of the electorate to which the politicians are responsible. Though the foregoing account of two-party democracy is oversimplified, it is sufficient to suggest that our country would work somewhat better if, in the Congress, there were more party discipline. Then the parties would have more of an incentive to make a country work than do individual congressmen, or than the special interests from whom the congressmen get their campaign contributions. We can see, in other words, the benefit of strengthening our political parties. This conclusion is not at all new, but I believe I have provided a fresh justification for it. Strengthening American political parties is desirable because it gives politicians a reason, in their own self-interest, to make the society work better.

Section IX

I wouldn't want to push the argument that I have made too far. I wouldn't want to pretend that any reform, no matter how drastic and well designed, would create a society where everyone, whether a politician, the head of a firm, or an ordinary citizen, would *always* work for the benefit of the society as a whole. I don't believe it is within the wit of man to work out a society where *everyone, always* has a compelling interest to act in a way that is ideal from the point of view of the society.

It might be useful to go back to my trivial example about getting directions for free. However prosaic and unimportant this example is, it nonetheless tells us that no matter how much we worked at it, we couldn't set up a market which would work so well that people would *efficiently* get directions for pay! The cost and trouble of the transactions needed to sell directions to those who are lost would often exceed the amount paid. Moreover, the amount one should pay the person who gave the directions is something one would know only after finding out whether the directions were right. But, by then, the source of the directions would be some distance back and couldn't be paid. There are many circumstances, in government and outside of government, where even with the best knowledge in the world we can't put forth a perfect structure of incentives.

So there is, after all, still a need for the morality that the preachers have been advocating for these many millennia. There is plenty of work left over for morality, even after we improve the structure of incentives. Indeed, there is so much work left over for morality that there *still* isn't morality enough to go around! Morality is in short supply, even though our society also uses incentives. Obviously, then, morality is, indeed, a scarce resource. It follows that we should structure incentives so that we do not need to call on morality any more than we have to.

REFERENCES

1. See my *The Logic of Collective Action* (Cambridge, Mass.: Harvard University Press, 1965).

2. See, for example, Talcott Parsons and Neil Smelser, *Economy and Society* (Glencoe, Ill.: The Free Press, 1956)

3. James E. Sheridan, *Chinese Warlord: The Career of Feng Yhu-hsiang* (Stanford: Stanford University Press, 1966).

4. Edward Banfield, *The Moral Basis of a Backward Society* (Glencoe, Ill.: The Free Press, 1958).

5. See my *Rise and Decline of Nations* (New Haven: Yale University Press, 1982).

6 : 2

SELF-INTEREST AND SOCIAL MOTIVATION

Howard Margolis

The characteristic approach of economists (and of political scientists, sociologists and philosophers influenced by the elegance and pragmatic success of the economic paradigm in the context of markets) uses two assumptions which strike me as very dangerous for the project of trying to build social theory. One plays no overt role in Mancur Olson's argument, so I will just mention it and move on. But I will want to argue a bit with my friend on the second point. At the end, however, I will nevertheless endorse a good deal of what he writes, for he is a founder of the "public choice" school of social analysis, and I am an only slightly disloyal follower.

The assumption I want to mention in passing has to do with the economist's usual practice of taking tastes for granted. Individuals are assumed to be guided by their tastes, which in turn are treated as autonomous—just a matter of what each individual happens to like. But everyone, including economists, knows that tastes are powerfully shaped by the social setting in which an individual acquires his or her tastes. So we have an assumption (like the self-interest assumption which will be our main concern) which is convenient and generally harmless in the analysis of markets but which quickly becomes perverse in the context of politics and social theory, where so much that is important consists of circumstances and deliberate efforts which influence tastes and reshape preferences. It is a separate story how societies generate tastes. Fortunately, I don't have say anything about that, because Michael Arbib has already given an effective and entertaining account of the main points that have to be considered.

The other assumption, the one I want to discuss in some detail, will be familiar to you even if you are not an economist. It is customary in economics to analyze things in terms of self-interest. But there are both strong empirical and strong theoretical reasons for supposing that man is indeed a social being, and that human motivation is a *mixture* of self-interested and socially motivated behavior. This is not in fact a very controversial claim, and in recent years in particular we have seen a good deal of work exploring this theme. (See, for example, Etzioni 1988 and Frank 1988. My own view is spelled out in Margolis 1982.) Olson is explicit about this point, making clear that social motivation—morals, ethics, norms, or whatever label you wish to use—is not to be ignored as a possible source of behavior. But here Olson follows what has become the usual line on this matter, which allows for social motivation but only, so to speak, lets it in the back door. Yet—and this is the main point I will try to develop—it requires a strong and I think empirically implausible separability condition to suppose that we can analyze human choice in social contexts in terms of self-interest, and only then allow for social motivation—or moral motivation—as something extra to be let in as fallback, something that is outside the main analysis, to accommodate things that can't be squeezed into terms of self-interest.

If we go back far enough, to the Scholastic analysis of markets from which today's economics slowly emerged, an analogous situation prevailed. The precursors of our economists concentrated on supply and mostly ignored demand. Instead of analyzing interactions of supply and demand, both of which played a role in determining price—as we take for granted today—analysis proceeded as if supply alone governed. People came to market with a certain amount of money to buy (say) grain. The price was then just a matter of spreading that fixed amount across the supply of grain brought to market. But not even the most elementary treatment for beginners would analyze things that way today. No one would think it useful—even as a simplifying assumption—to organize a study of markets in terms of supply effects only, and then bring in something about demand only if things could not be worked out. There are all sorts of particular contexts in which demand can be taken as fixed—but no one would suppose that is the sensible base case to train your thinking about how markets work.

It seems to me that we have an analogous situation here in the social context. If we analyze everything in terms of strict self-interest and then include some social motivation only if we get stuck or if there is something left over, it is not likely to lead to nearly as powerful a social theory as if the two things are built in at the base of the analysis, as we do for supply and demand in standard economic analysis.

Here are two examples in which the narrow point of view seems to be inadequate, and the broader point of view helps us to understand things. These are essentially the positive and negative sides of the same issue. If you analyze things in terms of strict self-interest, it is very hard to understand some of the most elementary facts of social life. A standard puzzle that has been debated for thirty years is how to explain, in terms of the theory of rational choice, why people bother to vote. It is easy to do a calculation and to conclude that the probability that you will be killed while driving to the polls ordinarily must exceed the probability that your vote will determine the next president. So how could it be in your self-interest to bother to vote? Economists are quite familiar with that paradox. The puzzle has been known a long time; how is it to be explained? It's not that there is no explanation, but that there are a dozen, each believed (at most) by its proponent. There is no *generally accepted* rational-actor explanation of even such a fundamental feature of social life and politics as that people bother to vote. It seems to me that we should use a twenty-five-year rule for problems of this sort. If there is a simple and fundamental problem that a field has wrestled with for at least twenty-five years without getting anywhere, there is reason to consider the possibility that something is wrong in the basic point of view, that something is defective in the framework within which the analysis is being made.

The real significance of this puzzle with a self-interest, rational-action account of why people bother to vote is not so much voting itself. Voting does not take much of our resources. But how people vote has large social consequences, and it seems implausible that *how* people vote is independent of *what* makes them vote in the first place. Although voting itself doesn't take a great deal of resources, how people vote is certainly critical for the allocation of large amounts of resources. Merely "taking care" of voting by letting in a bit of social motivation at this point, or by saying that people just like to vote, doesn't really clarify the important issue of how voting affects social outcomes. We can get people to the polls by invoking a social "duty to vote but this gives us no clue to what they do once they have gotten there. Bothering to vote is just the beginning of a whole series of things that go on in society that involve voluntary contributions. People contribute to public television, often help others in trouble, and in time of war or oppression do very much more expensive and dangerous things. So an account of how such social motivation works, and how it interacts with the very evident role of self-interest in governing our behavior, is an essential feature of understanding how societies work. The issue goes far beyond accounting for the miniscule resources involved in taking the trouble to vote. The only other puzzle of comparably fundamental importance, it seems to me, is the other point mentioned at the start of these comments: understanding how individual preferences are socially shaped. How does it come about that "everyone knows" certain things, especially when what "everybody knows" about something is sometimes very different in another society, or even in the same society at an earlier time?

I think the key to understanding the interaction between self-interest and social motivation lies in noticing that human beings appear most comfortable—seem to be in equilibrium—when they feel *neither selfish nor exploited*. This shows up in the phenomenon I call "incomplete coercion This is the opposite side of the voluntary-contribution issue. It turns on the point that no society could work if it had to depend wholly on coercion to assure compliance with the law. No society could function well if the people only obeyed the law to the extent that obeying the law served their rational self-interest, or only to the extent that they were coerced to comply. Every society depends on people usually being willing to obey the law even when it isn't strictly in their self-interest to do so. The income tax in every society (very clearly so in our own society) depends a good deal—not solely, of course, and probably not even mainly, but a good deal, nevertheless—on what the IRS itself calls "voluntary compliance The IRS is quite aware that the formal deterrents to tax evasion are by no means enough to get the degree of compliance that we have. For taxes, and for laws in general, the costs of policing-the burden on the society due to law enforcement—would explode if not for the fact that most people, most of the time, are doing pretty much what the law requires, even if there is no policeman nearby.

So on the one hand, the way societies operate depends on a certain amount of voluntary social behavior, like voting. On the other hand, every society depends on incomplete coercion, on people being willing to comply with social rules and laws more than strict concern with their self-interest would lead them to do.

But putting meat on this skeleton—giving a structured account of the "neither selfish nor exploited" intuition—so that we can say something about the limits of voluntary action and incomplete coercion, and the circumstances under which such effects are particularly important or particularly weak—requires an account in which self-interest and social motivation are locked together in a common framework, as with supply and demand in the analysis of markets. I cannot go through that argument here. The only point I can make is the simple one that if behavior turns on an interaction between a distaste for being too selfish yet also a distaste for being exploited—even for a good cause—then an account that starts by cramming everything that looks like it could possibly fit into the self-interest corner, and then shoving whatever is left over into another corner, labelled "social" or "moral" is not likely to be adequate.

The story Mancur Olson told of the bandit-king makes sense to all of us who were brought up in a society in which democratic government is taken as the norm. We live in a society in which it simply wouldn't occur to us that a bandit-king, or any other sort of autocratic ruler, is better than a democracy. When Mancur tells a story which tells us that what we already believe is true, that sits quite well with us. But let me give you a strict self-interest argument that goes the other way, which may suggest to you that the self-interest theory by itself doesn't tell you much, since the theory turns out to be so malleable that you can lead it to whatever conclusion your *ex ante* prejudices make palatable. Suppose that I argue that a bandit-king is really likely to be better than a democracy. After all, we have examples of really nasty dictators, like Stalin and Hitler. They did great harm. But they did not merely rob their countries blind for personal gain. I never hear it claimed that Hitler lived terribly extravagantly, or extravagantly at all, compared to the Queen of England. You never hear remarks about how expensively Stalin lived. The reasons why we are upset by Hitler and Stalin have nothing to do with exploiting their people for private gain. The problem with Hitler and Stalin doesn't seem to be explained by the bandit-king story: certainly not unless you first see what happened and then define the leader's interest to be whatever he turned out to try to do, so that is a tautology that the leader was always acting to maximize his own interest. Indeed, you can make an argument that a dictator who did act only in his self-interest would be powerfully constrained to be a very good sort of governor. Mancur gave you that version himself with the story about the man who was sure the Italian king would take good care of his property, i.e. of the country. In particular, the king would have good reason to want the country to thrive, to be united, to be convinced that what it needs is the kind of government provided by him. He knows that it can become very expensive to keep things running so that he has plenty of taxes if people are resentful or angry about what he is doing, and that he could lose everything he had unless he could maintain a reasonable degree of conviction that he is doing a good job in running things. So the bandit-king (in his pure self-interest) might be powerfully motivated to do a good job for the country.

On the other hand, in terms of purely self-interested behavior by leaders and followers, you might have a much worse situation if you had a democracy, because, in a democracy the ruler has to worry not just about doing a good enough job to avoid losing control, but also about keeping his majority. So in a democracy there might be, on the theory of strict self-interest motivation, quite a divisive incentive in which the ruler would pick out fifty-plus percent of the citizens and give them as much as needed to keep their support. Since fifty plus percent is a lot of people, he would be under much pressure to buttress his largesse with as much as he can take from the minority. In other words, the democratic ruler has some of the incentives of the bandit-king for running the whole country effectively, but that fact is going to be qualified, and perhaps devastated, by his concern to keep his majority solid, whatever the consequences might be for the rest of the country.

We can imagine a very smart Martian, told to analyze politics in a society he had never seen, where motivation is always purely self-interest; it is hard to see why he would find my account of the benefits of a bandit-king more plausible than Mancur's account of the benefits of democracy. There is only so much private aggrandizement a bandit-king could have the time and stamina to consume. But the democratic regime could do a great deal of damage before satisfying the appetites of its majority. Now in fact, democracies don't work that way. Democracies work in a different way because it is clear that people have powerful ties to their societies, not just to their private interests. People care not just about themselves (though, of course, they do care a lot about themselves) but also about their societies. This sometimes takes forms we admire, but sometimes it takes perverse forms, and sometimes it takes forms that we merely find puzzling. To understand what is going on we need to understand how self-interest *interacts with* social motivation, and the cognitive dynamics of persuasion and belief.

An example that might stimulate you to think about what goes beyond strict self-interest is Mrs. Thatcher's response to the invasion of the Falkland Islands. In terms of self-interest there is no question about what the appropriate response of England to the Argentine invasion was—to say "to hell with the Falkland Islands After all, there were very few people there and the Argentines were already in possession of the place. It was going to cost a lot of money from people living in England to get the islands back. In terms of the rational self-interest of her constituents, the appropriate behavior for Mrs. Thatcher was certainly not to spend billions to retrieve those tiny bits of land off the coast of Argentina. And yet Mrs. Thatcher became a heroine in her country, much to the despair of her opponents, by leading the country to retake the Falklands. You cannot make any sense of that in terms of the self-interest of English voters as individuals. You can make a good deal of sense of it in terms of a people who are bound by a sense of an English community, an English nation. The response to what was perceived in England as unwarranted aggression and an insult to the nation was obviously seen by the English as saying something about who they are and what they are. But that is not the sort of analysis that fits very comfortably within a framework of narrow self-interest, unless it is an elastic sort of self-interest which can be stretched, *ex post*, to fit whatever happened.

Mancur Olson made the point at the beginning of his talk that he did not want to deny the significance of moral considerations in accounting for social behavior. But "morality is a scarce resource you can't have all of it you would want. So societies must rely a great deal on self-interest as the motivating factor even when the object is something on the social scale, like good government and a strong and efficient economy. Successful societies are ones that manage to structure things, to arrange institutions, so that to a large extent self-interest gives actors an incentive to behave in socially useful ways. That is a very important point. As Mancur put it, morality isn't the sort of thing that grows on trees. You can't just go outside and pick some more anytime you're running short. Societies need to economize on their reliance on morality, and the more things can be arranged so that self-interest motivates socially helpful behavior, the less burden is placed on that essential but limited resource, morality. But that resource, though limited, really is essential.

And yet *how* morality (social motivation) plays a role is not as some reserve—like a backup checking account you can use when the main account runs low—but as an aspect of human motivation that is always operating, somehow interacting with self-interest, where self-interest is also always operating. A deep account of how societies work needs to deal with that interaction, and indeed (I would argue) needs to be built up from a view of individual motivation that allows for the social component of human motivation on the ground floor, treating social motivation as something just as fundamental, and just as real, as the more obvious motive of self-interest.

REFERENCES

A. Etzioni, *The Moral Dimension.* New York: Basic Books, 1988.

R.H. Frank, *Passions within Reason.* New York: Norton, 1988.

H. Margolis, *Selfishness, Altruism & Rationality.* New York: Cambridge University Press. Paper reprint, Chicago: University of Chicago Press, 1984.

ASCENT AND DECLINE
OF A SELF-CENTERED CULTURE

Louis Dupré

The term culture has so many meanings that I could fill the entire allotted space by quoting definitions culled from various anthropological, sociological, and philosophical treatises. The anthropologist Ruth Benedict summarizes many of them in her succinct but comprehensive formula, "a more or less consistent pattern of thought and action." Indeed, culture includes all the ideas, norms, values, rules of conduct, and expectations prevalent in any given society.[1] Through culture the person defines his place with respect to his cosmic and social environment, but also with respect to what he or she perceives as transcending both. Culture so described as a fact is an ever-changing process, a constant dialogue, an endless quest.

But precisely its dynamic nature also makes culture into an ideal, a goal to be pursued. No general descriptions are available to describe these goals, for they differ substantially from one culture to another. What renders the differences significant is that they also determine the content. This appears clearly in what we with an all too comprehensive term refer to as "Western culture Despite an unquestionable continuity of concepts, modes of expression, even of partial ideals, the teleology of the process substantially changed at several points. Two major changes occurred when the point of gravity was transferred from the Greek to the Roman world, and when the entire Greco-Roman culture was transformed by Christianity. Here I shall deal only with a third, perhaps less dramatic but no less substantial, change at the beginning of the modern epoch. What had previously consisted in an attempt to find one's assigned place in the totality of things and to attain a harmonious relation with a cosmos which supports as well as surpasses the ephemeral human construction, now

turned into the far more ambitious attempt to define humanity independently of any "given" place.

For the Greeks and Romans of the classical age, as well as for
the Hebrews of the biblical epoch, the human person occupied a central and unique position in the whole of nature or creation. To ascertain this it suffices to reread the first stasimon of Sophocles' *Antigone*
or Psalm 8. Called to cultivate and, according to Genesis, even to
dominate all other beings, he is charged with bringing the cosmic harmony to perfection. Two common traits characterize these ancient
ideals: first, the elements to achieve the human task have been given,
and second, the person must submit to the larger totality of "nature" in
order to discover its intrinsic laws and norms. The Greek and Latin
terms that come close to our own concept of culture imply these distinctive traits: *paideia*, meaning education, and *cultura animi*, referring to the cultivation of what nature has entrusted to us. Nothing
could be further removed from either than an opposition between *nature* and *culture*. Nature consists not merely in what *actually* exists: it
also includes the past from which the present has resulted and from
which future states of affairs will emerge. Hence the concept functions both as a principle of process and as an actual process. The dynamic quality of this concept accounts, at least in part, for its
remarkable normative impact. Nature impels things to be, while di-
recting them toward their eventual *perfection*. Being first, it set the
standards for what is to come last. The ancient concept of nature,
then, at once ideal and empirical, refers to an all-comprehensive, yet
very definite, *order of things*. That order includes social structures,
codes of personal conduct, as well as theological theories and physical
laws. The Greeks of the preclassical and the classical period perceived
what is in the mode of necessity, that is, as *what ought to be*.

Inevitably, as the emphasis on the person's creative powers
increased, his relation to nature became more complex. Could one
really find rules for human conduct in nature, or did the creative act
include its own norms? This issue was already raised by the Greek
Sophists. The reaction of the Greek tragedians, and even more that of
Socrates, determined the answer for centuries to come. Even
Lucretius, arguing on the basis of the less rational Epicurean view of
nature, left no doubt that happiness lies in conforming one's aspirations to what nature yields, not in taking the initiative against her.
Now, the biblical idea of creation, adopted by Christians, attributed no
such overriding normative qualities to the physical world. To conceive of God as creating freely cannot but result in a contingency of
finite being incompatible with the notion of form, central to the Greek
mind. Aristotle's "matter" now ceases to function as an intrinsic

determination of form and becomes instead that universal passivity of finite being which enables it to receive form, "So soon as nature is conceived to be created by God, the contingent becomes more than an imperfection in the embodiment of form; it is precisely what constitutes a natural object more than an embodiment, namely a creature."[2] Nevertheless, without being divine the world as handiwork of a divine Creator retains both an intrinsically religious and an ethically normative character. In a well-known passage (Rom. 2, 14), Paul ascribes to nature a normative quality as well as a revelatory power: "When Gentiles who do not possess the law carry out its precepts by the light of nature, then, although they have no law, they are their own law, for they display the effect of the law inscribed in their hearts." Reflecting the divine light, the world bears an intrinsic meaning of its own: "His visible attributes have been visible, ever since the world began, to the eye of reason, in the things he has made" (Rom. 1, 20). The human person thereby appears as "the image and glory of God" (1 Cor. 11, 7). But Christians, knowing that "the figure of this world was to pass away," felt disinclined to expect much ethical guidance from nature or to consider the world a serious object of religious contemplation.

Yet as the second coming was delayed, a more positive attitude toward nature developed. In the end, Christian culture proved remarkably capable of integrating the ancient concept of nature with the new life of grace. Looking then at the conception of nature that gradually developed within the Christian culture, we cannot but marvel at the surprising continuity which links it with ideas current in Rome at the end of the Republic.

Among them the Stoic ones dominated. They had already made their impact upon such biblical writings as Ecclesiastes and the Book of Wisdom, which presented the world as created by measure, number, and rule. Its order reflected the divine wisdom of its maker. One essential difference was, of course, that God remained *beyond* nature and that it depended on Him in its existence and even in its essence. This central contrast gave rise to a number of other, significant differences. Nevertheless, when we compare the traditional Christian cosmology to the modern, its continuity with the ancients is far more striking than its discontinuity. Christians also considered this world as one created by the rule of divine Wisdom. Its hierarchical order reflected the light of that Wisdom.

Nor is it true, as is often claimed, that for Christians the cosmos had ceased to play a significant theological role. Cosmological speculation abounds among the Church Fathers, in the East (Origen, the Cappadocians, pseudo-Dionysius) as well as in the West (Clement, Ambrose, Augustine, Isidore). Commentaries on the *hexaemeron* of

Genesis provided ever new opportunities for theorizing about nature—most of it in the tradition of Plato's *Timaeus* and Aristotle's *Peri Philosophias.*[3] The planets, for good or for bad, influenced the terrestrial events of birth and death, of character, success and failure. Even the great Scholastics admitted the instrumental causality of the stars upon sublunar events. Aristotle's *substantiae separatae,* the movers of the planets, were tentatively identified with the Judaeo-Christian angels, and the bodies of the elect were believed to possess the eminent qualities of *claritas, subtilitas, agilitas, impassibilitas* characteristic of the astral bodies.[4] A divinely established cosmic order determines man's place and prescribes the norms of his behavior (*cf.* Boethius and pseudo-Dionysius). Political structure had to conform to the cosmic hierarchy as Thomas's *De Regimine Principium* and Dante's *De Monarchia* unhesitatingly affirm. Even Plato's idea of an *anima mundi* was not simply discarded: several medieval theologians felt that the Holy Spirit could easily fulfill this function.[5] There was, to be sure, also a pessimistic streak in the Christian worldview. But even this may have been inspired as much by Greek (possibly gnostic) sources as by the biblical story of the Fall and by Paul's theology of original sin. In any event, it became solidly integrated with the Greek cosmological schema.

For the Greeks, the rationality of the cosmos had followed from its divine character and this had also been the case (though in a different way) for medieval theologians. A basic rationalism pervades all of Western culture and to it we owe the unique character of objectivity that connects the dawn of our civilization with modern thought. Yet an equally basic difference separates the ancient from the modern worldview. For the Greeks and medieval Christians, Arabs, and Jews, a rational logos, variously interpreted, *inhered* in the *given* nature of reality. It definitely did not emerge from a human mind imposing its own categories upon a world devoid of a rational necessity of its own.

It was, I believe, in the early Italian Renaissance that the idea of fostering and developing an existing potential started giving way to man's need to assert himself independently of nature's arrangement. He began to regard the entire socialization process as a construction of his own free will and insight. Only by surpassing his given humanity would he grow fully "human The mature expression of this is, of course, Pico della Mirandola's *Oratio,* in which he presents man as that Protean being that has no fixed nature of its own so that it is able to adopt all. Increasingly in the following centuries, culture came to consist in a refusal to accept nature as *given.* The term *humanitas* itself articulated an ideal, an invitation to lift oneself above ordinary mankind. What had once been a means for accomplishing one's assigned task now becomes an independent end in itself, an ideology.[6] In acquiring *humanitas*, man as the new creator of his nature rivals his divine Maker. The rebel Prometheus, the thief of heaven's fire, replaced the loyal Hercules as principal hero in the myth of culture.

Henceforth culture and nature become separated. The person no longer forms part of the cosmos, but uses and transforms it according to his means and needs. Thus begins that unprecedented emphasis upon the *self* as sole principle of meaning and value. Rationality ceases to be an objective quality inherent in the nature of things. More and more it comes to consist in the categories which the mind imposes upon a cosmos devoid of immanent reason. This move to the subject resulted in a rising opposition between an imperious subject and an amorphous world which it informed with its own rationality. The rational subject's mastery of this newly forged scientific method inaugurated an unprecedented upsurge of the physical sciences. It also reduced the real to what the subject can analyze and control. This subjectification of the rational culminated, of course, in Kant. With him, thought ceased to be intuitive contemplation altogether and became an operation of categorical structuring. We cannot imagine the Greeks, the medieval Scholastics, or even the rationalists of the modern age describing the cognitive attitude as that of "a judge compelling a witness to answer" (Kant). The change reflects the momentous impact of the experimental method of science upon the very concept of reason.

The "real" became reduced to the *objective*, that is, what was constituted by an autonomous subject. While the Greek *theoria* had required the soul to be purified from its passions before being lifted up to the divine act of contemplation, the subject now adopted an attitude of domination toward its object. Its supremacy culminated in the idea "that only what I am going to make will be real."[7] Overall reason acquired a practical orientation, even in its theoretical activity. Its task now became to bestow form upon a formless world. Constituted objectivity and practical control entirely replaced the conception of meaning and value *inherent* in a given reality. They ended the rule of contemplation and introduced that of fabrication which, as Hannah Arendt has argued, resulted in an unlimited instrumentalization of the world: confidence in tools, supremacy of the principle of utility, reduction of nature to a workshop for human tinkering.[8]

An immediate result of the new attitude is that nature no longer "reveals" itself as a reality that must be taken on its own terms. Instead, it becomes what we entrap and control as a calculable, predictable force. In being forced to answer only our own questions and to respond to our practical demands, it becomes a truncated reality. Theoretical and practical concerns meet in this new attitude. Indeed, modern science, though it originated independently of any technical interests and for two centuries created almost no technology, nevertheless prepared both the methods and the attitudes needed for technological development once other, primarily economic, factors had made it possible. It initiated that ordering of nature which by the end of the eighteenth century would explode into a technical revolution which has now come to dominate our entire lives.

Modern technology is a conquest of nature on man's own terms without regard for its immanent processes except for the purpose of exploiting them. But, above all, it has ceased to be a means. The world we inhabit has been built *by* technique and *for* technique. Even though technology renders unprecedented services, it is anything but man's handmaid. For the services, in a classical reversal of the master-and-servant role, have made their dominion irreversible. In our civilization everything has become *function* and nothing is *end*. Instrumentalism, once it succeeds in imposing itself, tolerates no ulterior teleology, but creates a closed circuit in which distinctions between ends and means collapse. Purpose and act coincide in the smooth functioning of the system itself. Indeed, man forms an essential part of what he, with wishful detachment, calls "economic" or "social processes." He has neither the desire nor the power to escape from a vise that seems so indispensable to his well-being. The technical imperative summons him as much as it summons all of nature and demands his full attention. Technology has become the very face of reality. The possibility of transcending it vanishes ever more rapidly. Hence the paradox noted by Hannah Arendt that in the age when man became most worldly (that is, most exclusively interested in subjugating the world), the world itself has lost all intrinsic meaning. It has become reduced to a mental abstraction. What started by being a pure *object* ends up being devoid of any substance, a mere projection of the subject. Everywhere man encounters only himself and his own fabrications in this closed, autistic universe. Yet Heidegger adds, nowhere does man encounter himself *in truth*, that is, in his own essence.

A subject solely responsible for conferring objective meaning upon a world drained of intrinsic (or God-given) meaning has no content of its own. Hence what started as a *pure* subject ends up being an empty subject. This became most evident during the reaction of Romanticism against an increasingly rationalist, objectivist culture. Romantic poets and philosophers attempted to liberate the self from its oppressive life-draining task of constituting an objective universe. The self claimed the right to be free of constrictive rules of reason and morality—in its own, uninhibited self. In Rousseau's *Confessions* (and even in Joyce's *Portrait of the Artist as a Young Man*), the individual self is, for the first time, deemed worthy of attention—independently of any religious or moral justification as had been the case in the classical autobiographies that Augustine and Marcus Aurelius wrote. Art became a means to self-expression. Yet here modern consciousness experienced what may well have been its most bitter disenchantment: the autonomous subject that had been so totally engaged in the task of bestowing meaning upon all things had no content left in itself. The self had become a monadic center of meaning and power unable to relate to itself in any other way than it related to its self-constituted objects. The new science of psychology conceived to understand the *subject*, in fact, succeeded only in reducing it to an *object* of observation and analysis, not essentially different from other self-constituted objects. Kolakowski put it well:

> It seems that once our world picture has been cleared of
> so-called anthropomorphisms, the *anthropos* himself disap-
> pears as well. The critique was carried out in order to
> achieve a scientific attitude; it results in self-defeat,
> though, for this attitude becomes then as baseless as any
> other. It was defined with reference to the goals of knowl-
> edge, yet no goals can be defined in scientific terms.

Modern writing bears ample evidence of this death of the subject. There is, of course, the antihumanism of the various structuralist objectivist movements which, in an author like Foucault, results in a genuine hostility to man. But the phenomenon dates much further back. In his now famous essay on *The Dehumanization of Art* (1925), Ortega y Gasset showed how under the most diverse appearances modern art reveals an identical aversion to the human person. What Ortega describes here is not merely an attempt to restore a balance after the (failed) subjectivist experiments of the nineteenth century. It expresses a novel sense of defeat encountered in the attempt to return man to the central place he had occupied in the universe of meaning since the Renaissance. The new awareness had been anticipated in Nietzsche's vilification of the *religion of man* as a phenomenon of decadence and, even earlier, of Marx's absolute primacy of *praxis*. In them, Western thought reached the final stage of the development that replaced the intrinsic rationality of the world order by one of the subject's making.

Where formerly the subject had been the sole source of meaning and value, Marx took the principle of creativity one step further by including that subject itself in the productive act. For him, the subject, whether it be the empirical romantic self or the transcendental ego of

Kant's or Fichte's philosophies, no longer precedes the creative activity: it is the outcome of it. The motto of Goethe's *Faust*, "In the beginning was the deed," becomes quite literally the principle of that new way of thinking. Through his productive activity man creates both *himself* and his world. Thus Marx radicalized the modern rule that meaning and value are not *given* with the nature of reality, but are *constituted* by the living deed. It is the final triumph of Promethean thought. Culture originates from a succession of decisions by which we create, refine, and constantly revise a system of values. Even when speaking of its "inner dynamics," we must not forget that the inherent factors which determine its development are themselves the outcome of prior decisions and remain subject to subsequent acceptance or rejection.

Of course, I do not want to imply that a culture starts entirely anew at every moment. Its general tendency is to continue earlier trends. The longer they have existed, the more they become entrenched and the harder it is to change them. All this is common wisdom. But the continuity should not make us lose sight of the *reality* of conscious innovation. Thus choices made at the beginning of the modern age, though consistent with those of the preceding era, marked a genuinely new beginning. One particular potential came to be exploited at the expense of all others. Objectivity had been pursued since antiquity. But in the early Christian and medieval ages it had largely been balanced by an intensive inward trend which appears in the nature of art, the language of prayer, and, generally, the entire rhythm of life. To refer to God as the *Being* of the self (Eckhart) or its *super-essence* (Ruusbroec) is to move into a spiritual universe essentially different from that of the first cause or the perfect being which determined the predominant theology. Despite the presence of objectivist tendencies, the general orientation of earlier culture was not objectivist itself and remained open toward transcendence.

At the beginning of the modern era a decisive change of course took place. It is not merely that philosophy became increasingly object-oriented: to Descartes, God is primarily the "author of nature," the indispensable initiator of the mechanic process. But in the modern age philosophy would express the general drift of the culture more accurately than ever before. Descartes, Hobbes, and Spinoza articulated the ideas which dominated their age. The trend reached its natural conclusion in the deism of the seventeenth century and the materialism of the eighteenth and nineteenth centuries.[9] Countercurrents continued to react. Pascal rejected the Cartesian idea of God, while the French and Spanish spiritual writers simply ignored it. But the hub of modern life was elsewhere. The unqualified ideal of an objective science was to place its stamp on the entire culture.

Even such intrinsically subjective experiences as despair, loneliness, and anxiety were integrated within an objective psychology conceived on the model of physical causality.

> Such meaning-giving interpretations with qualitatively rich contents (as, for instance, sin, despair, loneliness, Christian love) were replaced by formalized entities such as the feeling of anxiety, the perception of inner conflict, the experiencing of isolation, and the 'libido.' These latter sought to apply interpretive schemes derived from mechanics to the inner experience of man. The aim here was not so much to comprehend as precisely as possible the inner contentual richness of experiences as they coexist in the individual and together operate towards the achievement of a meaningful goal; the attempt was rather to exclude all distinctive elements in experience from the content in order that, wherever possible, the conception of psychic events should approximate the simple scheme of mechanics (position, motion, cause, effect).[10]

Now a homogeneously objective universe is by its very nature valueless: it functions but leaves no space for any transcendent support of values. Values continue to be created but become reduced to historically conditioned preferences. This historicist objectivism affects all realms of culture. Whitehead pointed out in *Science and the Modern World* how it affects our sense of beauty.[11] The work of art becomes more and more a private expression of the preferences of a particular culture, at most a transitory and therapeutic diversion in the "serious business" of controlling the world. Systems of thought (with the exception of science) likewise become isolated and, for all their universal ambition, basically private. They increasingly succeed one another without inner necessity. Today it is almost accepted that psychology and anthropology should provide a substitute for the intrinsic coherence which philosophy used to provide. We live in a fragmented universe without support and without soul that tolerates only ephemeral ideas and transient values. Thus the interesting replaces the lasting, the controversial the true, the assertive the meaningful.

What can be done? No way leads back to the past. A culture can only move forward, though "forward" must not mean in the same direction. It appears to me that the two qualities most urgently needed are clearheadedness and patience, particularly with respect to the loss of transcendence in our culture. Nothing would be gained by the blind, unquestioning "turn to God" which evangelists so peremptorily demand. First we must be able to *acknowledge* the loss of transcendence. This is particularly painful to the believer who tends to hide his head in the sand of a past spiritual tradition in order to avoid the sight of his own atheism. Our predicament is due not to a lack of faith but to a lack of inwardness. To profess a belief in God and to observe certain rules of ritual and moral conduct is not sufficient to regain it. Faith itself is permeated by objectivism. What is needed is a conversion to an attitude in which existing is more than taking, acting more than making, meaning more than function—an attitude in which there is enough leisure for wonder and enough detachment for transcendence. Culture requires freedom, but freedom requires spiritual space to act, play, and dream in. Such a space is not provided by leisure alone: leisure itself becomes suffocating without spiritual content. The space for freedom is created by transcendence. What is needed most of all is an attitude in which transcendence *can be recognized again*. The question of actual faith is entirely secondary to the recovery of freedom by detachment from the purely objective.

REFERENCES

1.   I derive this paraphrase from J.J.A. Mooij: *De wereld der waarden. Essays over cultuur en samenleving* (Amsterdam 1987), and from Max Wildiers, who incorporates it in his own *Het verborgen leven van de cultuur* (Antwerp 1988).

2.   Michael B. Foster, "The Christian Doctrine of Creation and the Rise of Modern Natural Science," *Mind* 43 (1934), 464.

3.   On this subject the reader may consult Max Wildiers, *The Theologian and His Universe* (New York: Seabury, 1982), 19-35.

4.   Wildiers, op. cit., 47, 246.

5.   Tullio Gregory, *Anima Mundi. La filosofia di Gulielmo di Conches e la scuola di Chartres* (Florence, 1955).

6.   *Cf.* Joseph Niedermann, *Kultur, Werden und Wandlungen des Begriffs und seiner Ersatzbegriffe von Cicero bis Herder* (Firenze: Biblioteca dell'Archivum Romanicum, vol. 28, 1941), 31, 77-78.

7.   Habermas considers the Greek ideal to be directly responsible for the technocracy of the modern age (*Knowledge and Human Interests*, translated by Joseph McCarthy [Boston: Beacon Press, 1984], 304). The Greek emphasis upon the object's independence from the knower's immediate interests did indeed create the *possibility* of a value-free science, a necessary precondition for such a technocracy, but only after late medieval nominalism had eroded the axiological dimension of thought.

8.   Marxists are by no means alone in their criticism of pure theory. Thus Rudolf Boehm also holds the Greek ideal of "superhuman" purely theoretical knowledge responsible for the inhuman technology and technologized pace of life in our age. According to him, Descartes' separation of the *res extensa* from the *res*

cogitans, which reduced the self to the status of an empty subject and the world to a mechanistic object, merely drew the conclusions contained in the ancient notion of theory (Rudolf Boehm, *Kritik der Grundlagen des Zeitalters* [The Hague: Martinus Nijhoff, 1976], especially chapter 4).

9. Marx considered the French materialism of the eighteenth century the direct outcome of Descartes' and Locke's theories on the one hand and of Bayle's religious skepticism on the other. *Cf. Die heilige Familie*, in *Marx-Engels Historisch-kritische Gesamtansgabe*, ed. D. Rjazanov (Frankfurt, 1972), 1(3), 300-5.

10. Karl Mannheim, *Ideology and Utopia*, translated by Louis Wirth and Edward Shils (New York: Harcourt, Brace and World, n.d. [first edition 1936]), p. 17.

11. Alfred N. Whitehead, *Science and the Modern World* (New York: Macmillan, 1962), 174-75.

7 : 2

INWARDNESS AND INTERDEPENDENCE

William M. Sullivan

In "Ascent and Decline of a Self-Centered Culture", Louis Dupré has provided a remarkably concise and evocative account of the genesis of our most difficult cultural problems. Although its outlines are familiar, Dupré's narrative is not entirely easy to characterize. Its story of cumulative effects suggests a history of progress, while its stress on decisive discontinuities gives it a critical edge. There is also an unmistakable tone of elegy when Dupré recounts the continuity, subsequently lost, which classical and Christian thinkers found between nature and culture.

Although Dupré deplores the split of modern culture into disjoined inner and outer realms, he affirms the achievement of modern individuality as a cultural gain. So, while his narrative is certainly no brief for the progress of reason and science in the Enlightenment style, neither is it simply a nostalgic Decline of the West. On the other hand, Dupré's passionate complaint at modernity's loss of transcendence marks his account off from ironic affirmations of the current cultural situation in the chic postmodernist mode.

Irony is, however, the crucial point of the tale. After describing the conquests of modern objectivity as embodied in scientific technology even as it has overshadowed its source in the free but ultimately empty modern self, Dupré concludes that "our predicament is not due to a loss of faith but to a lack of inwardness."

This needed inwardness both is and is not the unlimited subjectivity which the Romantic thinkers have taught us is our true being. For Dupré, inner freedom is "created by transcendence. What is needed most of all is an attitude in which transcendence *can be recognized again.*" Or, as he has argued elsewhere, the only road beyond the empty subjectivity of modern culture is "the one opened by modernity itself: the inward road. Subjectivity after having damned our age may still turn out to hold its redemption."[1]

This sort of philosophical irony, in which the road toward a new integration lies through an intensification of the very forces which are destroying an older wholeness, recalls another theorist of modernity, G. W. F. Hegel. Dupré has made it clear elsewhere that he does not find the Hegelian solution of the problematic of modernity credible.[2] However, I think the Hegelian parallel—contrast—can be helpful in coming to grips with the challenge Dupré presents. He certainly is in agreement with Hegel that any way beyond the present culture of subjectivism must in some way go through and not around subjectivity.

As Dupré demonstrates, awareness of discontinuities makes a historical perspective essential for addressing the issues of modern culture. And I think we must also accept Dupré's claim that the subjectivization of modern culture is the crucial issue. However, I find no good reason why we must also accept our culture's usual self-understanding as valid in order to grapple with its problems.

Placing all our hopes in the further development of inwardness alone, as Dupré seems to counsel, seems to me highly dubious. This is, after all, precisely the line of development—stemming from Descartes—which, by Dupré's account, has helped seal us into the prison of subjectivity. For this reason, I think we can benefit from a strong dose of the Hegelian tonic: to seek possibilities for refloating subjectivity, not by hopelessly trying to abandon inwardness, but by grasping the self in the swim of contemporary society and history.

First, remember the lines of the Hegelian diagnosis of modernity and its possibilities. Individuality and subjectivity, to Hegel, were precious but ambiguous goods, the outcome of a conflictual and discontinuous history. Subjectivity was a gain in that it greatly enhanced human freedom and responsibility. It revealed a fuller dimension of humanity, as Christianity and the Enlightenment had in different ways affirmed.

On the other hand, the modern growth of subjectivity represented a loss of coherence in all dimensions of human existence. In its extreme manifestations this very subjectivity cut persons off from the sense of participation in the intrinsically meaningful, the transcendent. Thus Kierkegaard and Nietzsche, Weber, Heidegger, and Dupré. But for Hegel the same historical forces which were driving these developments—science, the market economy, and the modern system of nation states—were also opening up possibilities for a new, more complex integration of life. Hegel argued that, for all its darkness, modernity represented an important new dispensation in history.

The Hegelian strategy, if I may use that term, was to bring the highly individuated modern self into a meaningful social and ethical universe. The means to this end was to be participation in institutional and cultural life, from family, occupation, and politics to the realms of art, religion, and philosophy. The distinctively modern feature of this project was Hegel's awareness that it had to proceed in a manner appropriate to modern subjectivity, that the emerging civilizational order had to be freely chosen and consciously shaped. He thought this possible because he was convinced that the virtues of the emerging integration, not to say its necessity, could be made compelling through the public medium of philosophical persuasion. In this way the goods of modern subjectivity were to be both embraced and transcended toward a wider vision of life.

As its subsequent exponents have seen, the Hegelian project affirms the inescapably public and thus, in the broad sense, democratic nature of an authentic modern culture.[3]

It also affirms the centrality of subjective inwardness through the public recognition of individuality in institutionalized human rights, especially rights of participation. For this reason, an adequate modern cultural order requires that individuals understand their situation and the history which has produced it, including its conflicts. Reciprocally, ethical self-awareness, along with its concomitant responsibility, can only be developed fully through participation in common deliberation. Individuals become autonomous in their ability to affirm reflectively the reasonable goods of public deliberation and assume responsibility for this process.

But, given the disarray of modern culture, particularly religious and political life, is not this strategy utopian, even more than Dupré's project of a renewal through pure inwardness? Of course, it may be. But there are also developments in the contemporary world which strongly suggest its continuing relevance. To develop the contrast with Dupré, I want to sketch briefly a way in which what I have called the Hegelian strategy can be important.

As we near the end of the twentieth century, we are confronted by an overwhelming fact. Despite the enormous destructiveness of its wars and the off-the-scale dimensions of the totalitarian horror, the human species has grown vastly more interconnected. And not only interconnected: the world's peoples are now deeply dependent upon one another for their livelihood and even their survival. Both the terrifying codependence created by nuclear weapons and the deepening interdependence of the world economic order are becoming more evident daily, not only to experts but to average citizens, even to national leaders.

At the same time, and partly in response to the bewildering changes these developments are causing at all levels of society, a host of new ethical demands have arisen. Calls for transnational human rights, for solidarity in the face of natural disaster and human oppression, have mounted in frequency and intensity. Something like an international public opinion is becoming increasingly effective. Consider, for example, the campaigns against apartheid, the work of organizations such as Amnesty International, or support for Poland's Solidarity movement. Through all these there is manifest a growing awareness that we share a collective responsibility for the effects our increasingly powerful and interconnected activities have on the human and natural environment. Figures from Mikhail Gorbachev to Pope John Paul II have been sounding similar themes, and with considerable effect. As in Hegel's time, these developments are propelled by apparently autonomous and generally unplanned developments in science, technology, the economy and international politics. But the vast increase in scale and scope of these developments today is severely straining the capacities of both the institutional and cultural patterns of the modern order. Problems of global pollution, nuclear proliferation, economic competition, and ethnic hostility press the boundaries of the logic of self-interested action which has served as modernity's standard theory of human society. The time seems more than ripe for a compelling cultural vision which can serve to focus public argument and institutional experimentation. What might it look like?

In recent decades the emergence of ecology from a peripheral to a central position in both expert and popular awareness may hold great promise. As a general metaphor for the contemporary human situation, ecology suggests how to conceive the self-limitation of the global systems of technology, economics, and politics as a necessary response to interdependence.

The dangers inherent in our capacities to annihilate each other have become clearer since 1945. But a hopeful new recognition has been developing as well. Stephen Toulmin has described it as the realization that "the activities of human beings, their scientific activities as much as any other, have at last become significant elements within the operations of nature: in some cases, critical and controlling elements[4]

The key to this understanding is that since the human species is so involved in a great many ecological processes, these processes cannot be treated simply as objects for detached theoretical study—or equally detached technological manipulation. As Toulmin has argued, the central biological term, adaptation, "has an inescapable ethical component." The central question, both for science and for practical life, thereby changes. It can no longer be just, "How are human beings (passively) adapted to the natural habitat?; it is also, How are we (actively) to adapt ourselves to that habitat?"[5] This new question transcends the division Descartes and Bacon established between the knowing subject and passive nature. Along with that division the ecological understanding also calls into question the self-evidence of the modern division between inside and outside, culture and nature.

The resulting interdependence of human well-being and the planetary ecosystem forces us, at the price of survival, to respect and care for the whole of which we are a part. But then the typical modern identification of reason with calculative and strategic thinking becomes open to question. A rationality appropriate for ecological citizenship cannot maintain a rigid separation between scientific and ethical thinking.

The requirements of an ecological rationality demand relearning, under new conditions, something close to the classical and medieval understanding of the interrelation of theoretical and practical reason, in which knowledge and choice are guided by a search for the good of the whole. Toulmin concludes his case with the claim that a coherent ecological rationality demands a reverence for the integrity of the world as a regulative ideal.[6]

I want to underscore the Hegelian irony in the situation. Awareness that we are inextricably involved in a natural order which transcends our efforts to understand and control it is being forced upon us by our very attempts to extend our subjective will to dominate. In its drive to conquer the world, modern subjectivity is being brought to realize its limits. This impending crisis holds the possibility, even the necessity, of a new recognition of transcendence. That is, we find that it makes less and less sense to think of ourselves as, in Descartes' phrase, "the masters and possessors of nature Instead, we need to learn to think and act as participants within the greater whole of an encompassing cosmos.

To complete the picture, I would need to extend this line of reflection to the complex institutional, political, and cultural changes which the ecological metaphor suggests. But this is a task for another time. For now I hope the outlines of the counterposition to Dupré's position are clear. First, inner and outer are always interconnected (dare I say dialectically?). As Dupré's history also shows, culture is internally related to institutions. Second, it follows that cultural change cannot be understood apart from the whole story of how our species has developed and taken up its dwelling on this planet. Such an account need not entail a philosophical commitment to materialism. Third, while the difficulties confronting the position I have tried to sketch are enormous, they do not rule out hope.

To refer once again to Hegel's project, it is significant that he identified his much-disputed "cunning of reason" as a secular statement of divine providence. On the one hand, the tortuous evolution of the species was a struggle to respond to divine initiatives; seen the other way, the emergence of good from apparent evil showed the extraordinary willingness of the divine to meet human need on its own terms. Perhaps the point is better captured by a story from the Talmud related by the novelist Chaim Potok. A king once had a son who journeyed into a far away country. The king sent ambassadors to his son, imploring him to return. Finally, the son sent back word that he could not return. "All right," responded the father, "come as far as you can. I will go the rest of the way to meet you."

REFERENCES

1.   Louis Dupré, "Alternatives to the Cogito," *Review of Metaphysics* 40 (June 1987), 712.
2.   Ibid., 712.
3.   I mean Hegelian in the broad sense of drawing inspiration from Hegel's design. The neo-Hegelians such as T.H. Green in Britain, as well as Americans such as Josiah Royce, John Dewey, and George Herbert Mead exemplified this strategy. So do contemporary theorists such as Charles Taylor and, in the most encompassing way, Jürgen Habermas, to name only a few. The imprint of the Hegelian design is also apparent in the structure of the very differently conceived project of Alasdair MacIntyre.
4.   Stephen Toulmin, *The Return to Cosmology: Postmodern Science and the Theology of Nature* (Berkeley: University of California Press, 1982), 252.
5.   Ibid., 267.
6.   Ibid., 271-73.

DISCUSSION

Wilfred Ver Eecke (Philosophy, Georgetown): Professor Dupré, you indicated the difficulty that culture encountered in going toward the subject ultimately might call for reincorporation of religion. Would it not be possible to argue that the difficulties that culture encounters by going into the subjective domain will be solved by countermoves in that domain, rather than by going toward religion? Let me give an example; Professor Olson has written a book called *The Logic of Collective Action* in which he demonstrates, in the economic domain, that going purely in a subjective direction does not maximize what economists want to do. But economists do not move toward religion; rather they propose an economic strategy involving a "general public One could point toward the emergence of antitrust legislation as an example in the economic domain as to how the rights of the individual producer may be violated in the name of the collective benefit of the market. And thus one could suggest that it might be useful to have a reintegration of religion, but that does not seem to be what is going to matter for the culture itself.

Dupré: This gives me an opportunity to point out the one-sidedness of *my* talk. My talk was basically critical, not really more than that. I added an appendix in which I tried to indicate the indispensability of a few things for the future. One was a transcendent dimension; the other thing was (a point that was well developed by Professor Sullivan) that we have to go through the *existing* situation. Now I was not interested in speaking of religion as such. In fact, if I may be irreverent about it, being an aspiring pious person myself, I would say there is far too much talk about religion—we are not ready for it. To prepare an attitude of transcendence we first have to really do our homework and create an attitude of reverence, [cultivate] all the natural virtues that are the preparatory ground for religion, and which we somehow have lost. So [my talk] was not a plea or an apology for religion at all; in fact, if anything, I would say it is a bit premature for that.

This also gives me an opportunity to say a word about the difference between Professor Sullivan's suggestions and my own. When I spoke of having to deal with what we have, with a scientific, objectified concept of nature, with the human subject, with the turn to the subject, I only indicated one thing, namely, that one of our tasks is to try to give meaning, to give content, to that subjectivity itself. Now this is only half the task; Professor Sullivan was quite right in pointing out that this was not sufficient. He indicated the other part when he said that subjectivity must come to realize its own limits. That's where transcendence will be. In other words, in the scientific project as we have seen it developed, we will reach a new limit of that much-heralded subjectivity as a source of meaning and values; we will run up against our own boundaries and thereby we will encounter limits. I think *that* part of transcendence is important. I agree that, in other senses, there is already plenty of "religion" around.

8 : 1

AUTONOMY AND SOLIDARITY:
A NEW POLITY FOR AN OLD WORLD

Monika K. Hellwig

What yet remains to be said? We have discussed the progress of science, of technology, of ideas, and the effects that such progress has on the future of human life. We have looked at the discernible designs and patterns of our universe—those that are given, those that are humanly made, and even those that spring from human intervention but take on a spontaneous development of their own. We have looked at such designs and such auto-patterning at the physical, chemical, biological, psychological, and sociological levels of organization and activity. But what emerges most clearly is that the knowledge which we call science and the skills and machines which we call technology are not sufficient to resolve the increasingly urgent questions of human survival and well-being. We are faced with the shaping of values, of goals, of personal and social decisions, and of real commitments.

It is at this point that the question of human survival and well-being becomes, in the broad sense, a theological one. The question becomes one of the ultimate horizon of human hope, the ultimate reference point for the meaning of human existence, and the ultimate grounding of the determinants of human obligation. It is only at this level of questioning that one might hope to find an authentic solution to problems of plurality as these affect human lives—the problems inherent in the tension between freedom and community, autonomy and solidarity. As other papers in this volume have pointed out, we are rapidly approaching the dilemma of the sorcerer's apprentice. Tempted to rely on the formidable powers of technology which we have unleashed as the solution to our human problems, we find that we are on the threshold of developments in which the technology may escape our control and reshape the world in unpredictable and undesirable ways.

The question has been raised whether the subordination of the human race to self-evolving computer technology is necessarily an evil. But one might counter with the question whether behind every self-evolving machine there is not human origination by someone who wants to achieve something, wants power to accomplish something, perhaps wants power over other human persons as well as the resources of the universe. In the last century John Henry Newman was at pains to point out that while ideas might have a convenient business address in books, they actually resided and lived and produced progeny in their home environment in living, feeling, thinking people. In our own century we might extend that insight to insist that power may have its business address in machines, but that the goals and directions of that power have their original native ambience in human designers. And there is a responsibility that resides in the human initiator that cannot be lightly disclaimed by appeal to the complexity of the machines produced. There is no escape in reality from the question whether we shall use our great power against one another or in world community, to launch human and world destruction or to preserve and enhance.

In our own day, perhaps more sharply than at any previous time in history, the task of human survival and well-being confronts us with a challenge to examine our evaluation of autonomy and solidarity and our perception of the polarity between them. As Professor Dupré's paper has reminded us, the practical as well as the intellectual history of the modern Western world has revealed that a human culture based on intensive individualism is doomed, and is indeed already failing. A self-centered culture is one in which values and goals are privatized, and such a culture is judged and found wanting in the era of expanding population, massive increase in technical knowledge and power, and consequently elaborate patterns of interdependence in a seemingly shrinking universe. We are challenged to consider whether the valuing of persons can be distinguished from individualism, self-centered culture, and the privatization of values and goals.

To such questions about human possibilities a Christian anthropology, rooted in the biblical imagery and narrative, has much to say. The Christian response is not, of course, the only one that has a message for today, but it is one that is as viable in the complex circumstances of our time as it has ever been. And the first question to be addressed is the same as it has always been: whether human life and the world in which it takes place are ultimately meaningful or ultimately absurd. The question is consequential in the highest degree; if meaning is not given in reality, choices and actions are in the last analysis arbitrary, morality is reduced to utility or convenience, science is a matter of projection and chance, human society is the product of bargaining out of self-interest producing a frail and superficial harmony, and there is no guarantee that a genuine community of interest among human beings can be found.

Such a negative evaluation of human possibilities is not a casual fancy. In ancient times it was expressed vividly in a polytheism of hostile forces, allowing no possibility of resolution into harmony. More subtly, such a perspective reappeared in Gnosticism, reducing reality to binary conflict soluble only by annihilation of the material, the contingent, the individuated, the plural. Analogously, such a perspective also appeared in the extreme forms of post-World War II existentialism, in which the precarious freedom of the individual, in inevitable conflict with other freedoms, completes its journey of frustration in the final frustration of death. In the first of these forms, polytheism, there is no prospect of merging separate autonomies into solidarity of a universal kind. In the second, Gnosticism, there is ultimately only one autonomy possible, because solidarity is attained by the loss of plurality. In the third, extreme existentialism, autonomy has a momentary glorious existence swallowed up in tragedy because solidarity is not compatible with freedom.

The concrete simplicity of the narrative and imagery of the biblical creation stories should not mislead us. The interpretation expressed in them of the human situation is profound and bold. For the biblical narrator of the first and second chapters of Genesis, the meaning of reality is given, because all reality is gathered within a single horizon; there is no parallel force to challenge the creating One who calls and there is light and order, life and coherence. The narrative implies purpose in the calling of order out of chaos, and immediately locates the human person and community within the process: to be human is to be summoned into the likeness of the creating One, to order out of chaos, to harmony of the disparate, to community of enterprise. The narrative of the creation stories does not describe an event in the past, but interprets the continuing present of human experience in cosmos and time. The message, therefore, is of meaning and purpose *given* as constitutive of reality, and susceptible of human discovery and discernment. The grounds on which such a conviction rests cannot, of course, have a force other than that of Pascal's wager;[1] science and common-sense observation provide grounds of credibility for such a conviction, but in the nature of things it is a leap of faith, because we cannot stand outside of all reality to make judgments about the whole. What is to be said for the wager is that even if it is wrong it gives purpose to human existence, and courage and motivation to the project of human community, while the alternative is surrender to final despair without testing reality.

The assertion of meaning given as constitutive of reality is not yet the answer to the further question whether the universe is benign or indifferent to human existence. On this question biblical narrative and Christian anthropology are positive but quite cautiously nuanced. In the creation narrative the world is indeed given to human beings but with conditions attached. Combining the two versions of the story from the first two chapters of Genesis, one learns that human beings are to take possession of the world, consider it theirs, till and cultivate it, but respect the harmony and design by which various kinds of sustenance are given to various creatures, respecting also the center about which the whole interdependent system pivots, that center being the preserve or prerogative of the original creating One. Literally, of course, the story speaks of the fruit of a central tree that is not to be touched and which has to do with knowing good and evil.

Through the ages many interpretations have been given of this classic story so basic to biblical anthropology. But perhaps the deciphering of what it is that constitutes the forbidden fruit is not nearly as important as the acknowledgement that there are limits built into human freedom and creativity, and that those limits have to do with the centering of created reality on the creator. The actual play of the symbolism of the story is subtle. The human beings are called forth to be in the likeness of the creator, themselves in some sense creative, spontaneous, self-defining, autonomous; a drive in the direction of autonomy, self-definition, and world-definition is constitutive of their very being. The seduction that is introduced suggests that the way to fulfill that drive is to usurp the centrality that belongs exclusively to the creator. The message of seduction in the story sounds very much like the description of the self-centered culture of modern times which Professor Dupré described. The sequel of the seduction is that the whole project becomes impossible on those terms. Literally, in the words of the symbolic narrative, they are cast forth from the garden, the place of harmony, into an outer darkness of confusion and hostilities and difficulties, having discovered in a terrifying way their nakedness, that is, their vulnerability and individual fragility (Genesis 3).

It is clear that something is being said here about the continuing present of our existence, and about the terms on which it could be harmonious and satisfying, and finally about the way in which those terms are not being met. It is a story about freedom and dependence, about autonomy and plurality. It is an insight about the situated and conditioned character of human freedom or autonomy. That freedom is dependent on not putting the self at the center, because the self is incapable of sustaining that position, and simply implodes from the pressure, leaving anxiety, inauthentic relationships, and violence. Seeking correlation between the experiences of our worldly existence and the terms of the story, one might hazard the suggestion that the realistic limitation of human freedom that is being acknowledged has two dimensions. In the first place there is the necessary acceptance of the original givenness of one's own existence and of the universe, and of certain intrinsic patterns and limitations built into the given reality, not perhaps as final limitations but certainly as the available starting points for human creativity. But in the second place there is the crucial practical finitude of the freedom of each human person, constituted by the existence of multitudes of other human beings with the same needs for survival and sustenance and with the same drive to personal autonomy, to self-definition, and to world-definition.

Here, then, is the key question of autonomy and solidarity. If the human drive for freedom, creativity, self-definition is not a cruel joke, an inbuilt longing that must founder upon the twin rocks of worldly facticity and the plurality of free beings in inevitable interdependence, on what terms can such a drive for freedom be realized? The bold answer of biblical and Christian anthropology is that human freedom is in the last analysis fulfilled precisely as a creaturely or responsive freedom, and that true human freedom is reached finally as a communal freedom—not collective, but communal, dependent on networks of interdependence. There is an important implication here that freedom or autonomy cannot be defined in a static way, but has to do with process. As Nicolai Berdyaev was wont to point out, the uncreated freedom of the beginning is precious only because it is the starting point for the journey toward the consummated freedom of the end, the full commitment to what is fully worthy of the commitment. The uncreated freedom of the beginning is lodged in the self-assertion of the individual, but the consummated freedom of the end is possible only as the joint possession of interdependent persons in an interdependent universe of beings and powers which are ultimately grounded in a source that transcends them.

What all of this implies is that the universe in which we have our being is benign to human existence, rather than indifferent to it, but that it is benign precisely in presenting an inescapable exigence of uncentering the self, even the collective self of partisan interest groupings, in order to dedicate personal autonomy to the creation of a genuine solidarity. The extent of the solidarity demanded has increased with the technical and social complexity of our world, its expanding population and its proportionately shrinking resources. The dimensions of this have been well described in the incisive works of Wilfred

Desan,[2] while the urgency of it has preoccupied scientists in many fields. But a question that cannot be avoided, and which is again a theological question, is whether it is already too late, whether the possibilities of human and global solidarity have already been irrevocably spoiled by cumulative consequences of exploitation, domination, and reckless invention, and by massive aggregations of self-centeredness and collective implosion of cultures.

To this third question Christian anthropology again gives a nuanced answer. In the story as it unfolds in the third chapter of Genesis, return to Paradise is barred by an angel with a flaming sword. As a reflection on the continuing present of our worldly experience, this is an admission that our relationships with one another and with the transcendent source of our being are not, and never will be, characterized by innocent simplicity and spontaneity. Autonomy carries risk, and the autonomy of individuals who are inevitably interdependent in complex patterns carries a very complex pattern of risks for the entire human project. We have lived, and have experimented, have made mistakes and have overasserted freedom by ignoring the claims of others, of the ecology, and of the future, and we live now in the world as shaped not only by the original creation that continues in the continuing present, but also by the consequences of human action and experimentation. Such a world is both the outcome of the original blessing, and of the evolution of a subsequent curse, both a home and an exile, a place of ambivalence demanding critical discernment and re-creative action.

A Christian anthropology is, of course, not only Adamic in its vision of the human, but also Christic, grounding in the historical event of radical conviction about the transformations possible in a history seen as moving to a purposeful end. In the redemptive or transformative vision of the unfolding future, the growing power of scientific knowledge and technical capacity to make that knowledge effectively operative is necessarily seen under three aspects. In the first place, the unfolding possibilities share the goodness of all creation in its original blessing. In the second place, as instrumentality of human autonomy, they share the risks of human freedom inasmuch as they can be used to destroy, dominate, or divide, and it is observable that this has in many instances happened. In the third place, however, these possibilities of science and technology can be used redemptively as the means of new life and hope and community. In a Christian anthropology, therefore, the rapid growth in human knowledge and power is subject to scrutiny and evaluation, and *the primary criterion for such an evaluation must necessarily be the maturing of human autonomy into authentic patterns of solidarity.*

In the era since the Second Vatican Council in Catholic circles, and perhaps since the end of the Second World War in Protestant circles, a new awareness of the worldwide practical application of this criterion has come into focus.[3] The traditional assertion that the primary criterion is obedience to the law of God has been considerably diluted by the awareness that "nature" is not as static as once appeared, and that the "law of nature" is therefore not as univocally evident as it may once have seemed, while Scripture does not directly address many of the major problems of our time, and church authority itself must show whence its conclusions are drawn. While in principle, therefore, the primary criterion for judging the developing structures and activities of the world is the "will" of the creator, in practice it is necessarily the other term of the traditional couplet[4] that comes into play—the demand for human solidarity.

It is the pressure of this practical exigence that has aroused the voices of the so-called Third World to challenge traditional Christian anthropology out of its privatized modern frame of reference and out of its too easy affirmation of the developments of modern intelligence and inventiveness. The issue is not the highest possible development of human possibilities for some privileged few whose costs are borne more and more extensively and intensively by the many, but rather whether particular developments are progressively establishing effective human solidarity in resources, opportunities, and power. Such solidarity cannot be bought at the expense of autonomy by the subjugation of many to the domination of the few, in spite of the fact that this would seem to be the more efficient way of bringing a certain unity and harmony to the world, and in spite of the increasing technical possibilities of such domination. The only truly human development toward world polity is one that restrains and harnesses technical power to serve authentic interaction of autonomous persons growing toward responsible and voluntary solidarity.[5] This has, of course, massive implications for the uncentering not only of the individual self, but of the collective selves of national sovereignty, racial and cultural supremacy, economic power and ideological structures.

We are in need of a radical vision for human survival—*a vision grounded in the exigence of the transcendent.*

REFERENCES

1. To live and act as though a benign, provident, and adequately powerful creator presides over cosmos and history is a wise wager, because nothing would be lost and much gained even if it should turn out that the assumption is untrue.

    2.   Most recently: *Let the Future Come* (Washington, D.C.: Georgetown University Press, 1987).

    3.   Examples of such concern are: Dietmar Mieth and Jacques Pohier, eds., *Ethics in the Natural Sciences* (Edinburgh: T. & T. Clark, 1989); and David Tracy and Nicholas Lash, eds., *Cosmology and Theology* (New York: Seabury, 1983).

    4.   Simultaneous and mutually inseparable love of God and neighbor.

    5.   Clearly, this necessarily includes ecological stewardship and compassionate reverence for all sentient life.

8 : 2

THE NEW SOLIDARITY:
HOW WIDE OUR WORLD?

Frederick Ferré

Monika Hellwig has beautifully drawn threads together while expanding our vision into ultimate theological questions. I aim to reinforce and extend this vision.

First, let me reinforce Professor Hellwig's approach to technology. Using a theological term deliberately pulled from its normal context, we can profit by looking at technology as *incarnational*. To incarnate something is (literally) to make it meat—or "flesh," if "meat" sounds too vulgar. In incarnation, meaning takes on matter. Incarnational vision sees in matter the meaning that matter embodies.

All technology embodies two kinds of meanings: value-meanings and knowledge-meanings. Every implement, tool, machine, device—from the simplest hoe to the most complex computer—embodies someone's judgment of value or disvalue. By considering the purpose behind the making of the artifact, we can discover what the maker considered worth pursuing or avoiding. We can see, embodied in matter, what sorts of things are not considered taboo. In a culture of strict religious vegetarianism, for example, we would not be likely to find instruments for the hunting of animals. The hoe, on the other hand, embodies a judgment that it is not illicit to cut into the surface of the earth.

The hoe also embodies knowledge-meanings. This need not be theoretical knowledge, as we would recognize it today. But whatever one's interests or aversions, no implement could successfully become embodied without at least some cognitive capacity. Simply valuing the eating of animal flesh, for instance, is not enough to provide the technologies of traps or weapons with which to pursue such values. Practical "know-how," at the minimum, is a necessary condition for technological embodiment; and in recent centuries theoretical "know-that" and "know-why," gained through the power of the sciences, has distinctively characterized the technologies of modernity.

An incarnational approach to the technologies surrounding us, therefore, will look closely at the two great necessary conditions to their embodiment: the value condition, without which nothing would be attempted, and the knowledge condition, without which nothing could be accomplished. Looked at this way, the world of artifacts around us cannot possibly be alien to the human. That world, our "technosphere," is constantly alive with human wants and human capacities.

This does not make our technosphere either easy to control, however, or easy to commend. Professor Hellwig notes that some patterns of our universe may be humanly made "but take on a spontaneous development of their own." She is right. It is far from easy to will just one thing. In choosing the convenience of private automotive transport, for example, we also choose—usually without awareness— the creation of massive highway systems, the destruction of neighborhoods, the development of "drive through" culture, the withering away of public transportation alternatives, and the esthetic blight of the "strip" with its malls, service stations, fast-food shops, and rusting junk yards. The "vertical integration" of technologies, together with the unknowable ramifications of every choice, means that technology, though human in its original purpose and implementation, seems autonomous. To incarnational vision, this seeming autonomy cannot be complete, since change of value or growth of knowledge will in due course make a difference. But to incarnational vision, flesh is real. Matter is no phantom to be wished away, as in some Docetic dream. Matter in motion has momentum, and in the short run human purposes, however noble and far-seeing, may be crushed by runaway forces humans have unleashed.

Still more sobering, however, is the realization that the word "human" is, in this context, far from an adjective of praise. The incarnational vision of technology begins not with some *a priori* theory of the human but with what is concretely embodied, and will therefore find human values often wicked and human knowledge often narrow and distorting. Thumbscrews and torture racks are incarnations (alas) of human values and knowledge. An incarnational approach to technology will quickly rediscover the Fall. This approach will speak of "human technical capacities" not only, with Professor Hellwig, in terms of "the risks of human freedom inasmuch as they can be used to destroy, dominate, or divide, and it is observable that this has in many instances happened," but also plainly in terms of sin. Redemption, as she rightly says, will also be part of the message; but redemption from what? Not from "risks," alone, that have "in many instances happened," but from profound structural evils, built up for thousands of years, still guarded and tended enthusiastically by the human race. Dare any of us claim exemption?

Some of these evils are turned systematically against fellow-humans, as Professor Hellwig eloquently states. The poor, whom we seem indeed always to have with us, bear the worst brunt of incarnated sin. In the industrialized countries, these are the people whose lungs, due to inequitable housing patterns, are forced to breathe contaminated air from the factories and power stations designed to provide the wealthy with their goods. These are the powerless ones who, in the conveniently aggregated totals of our cost-benefit analyses, are picked to bear the costs while we others reap the benefits. In the nonindustrial part of the world, whole peoples are subject to environmental destruction, economic dislocations, and cultural domination from the industrial, First World powers. As Professor Hellwig concludes, "the primary criterion" for a (positive) evaluation of growing human knowledge and power "must necessarily be the maturing of human autonomy into authentic patterns of solidarity."

Exactly so! But how widely must these authentic patterns of solidarity reach out? Thus far my effort has been to reinforce Professor Hellwig's vision; now, in conclusion, it is my aim to extend it even more decisively. Professor Hellwig seems ambivalent about the place of nonhuman creation in the moral scheme of things. She does not ignore the topic. She includes "the ecology" among the victims of overasserted freedom and exaggerated human autonomy. She even allows that the ecology has "claims" that, like those of others and of the future, have been wrongfully ignored. But in her concluding statement of goals she ignores all but the anthropic community in her call for solidarity. She writes:

> The issue is not the highest possible development of human possibilities for some privileged few whose costs are borne more and more extensively and intensively by the many, but rather whether particular developments are progressively establishing effective *human* solidarity in resources, opportunities and power.... The only truly human development toward world polity is one that restrains and harnesses technical power to serve *authentic interaction of autonomous persons* growing toward responsible and voluntary solidarity (emphases supplied).

Earlier, in her cautiously nuanced exposition of the Christian answer to the question "whether the universe is benign or indifferent to human existence," Professor Hellwig says that "the world is indeed given to human beings but with conditions attached." But by the time she reaches her conclusions, her commendable zeal for solidarity with other humans has led her to forget—or at least to omit—the goal of solidarity with the rest of the world and the "uncentering" conditions of our earthly dominion. The cattle in our feed lots, the veal calves in our pens, the chickens in our battery cages, the cats and dogs in our experimental laboratories cannot share in goals stated exclusively in terms of "the authentic interaction of autonomous persons." The living topsoil, the threatened rivers and oceans, the atmosphere—these are not even in principle included as claimants for solidarity as long as our final goals are put in such anthropocentric ways.

Our problem in finding the way forward to appropriate paterns of solidarity with the human and transhuman world is not simple, however, since our rejection of anthropocentrism must not slide into misanthropy, as some "deep ecologists" seem wont to do. Nor may we allow ourselves, in our quest for a larger than exclusively personal context of moral obligation, to relax our concern for the unique value of autonomous persons. An ethic of "organicism" alone is too easily distorted by the subordination of precious personal lives to the claims of some all-demanding whole. Organic life is notoriously wasteful of individuals. In that direction, unless we counter it with a healthy valuation of unique individuality, lies fascism. We must thread our way between the Scylla of self-centeredness and the Charybdis of totalitarianism. What is needed if we are to maintain proper balance between parts and wholes, defined both socially and ecologically, is an ethic of *personalistic organicism.*

It is not clear to me whether biblical narrative and traditional Christian anthropology are capable of undergirding something so radical and so new as seems to be needed today. Perhaps these narratives can be cleansed of their heavy encrustation with domination attitudes. Perhaps they can be found to support a solidarity with the natural order that goes beyond valuing it as merely resource and historical stage-setting for the human drama. If so, it will require much further work (and humility) from philosophers and theologians.

Professor Hellwig's concluding sentence was: "We are in need of a radical vision for human survival, and that is a vision grounded in the exigence of the transcendent." I conclude with a paraphrase that summarizes my response: We are in need of a radical vision for *world* survival, and that is a vision that must be grounded in the exigence both of the transcendent *and of the immanent.* We need, that is, a new incarnational vision with an appropriately incarnational ethic.

REFERENCES

1. See my *Philosophy of Technology* (Englewood Cliffs, N.J.: Prentice Hall Publishing Co., Inc., 1988), esp. chapters 1, 2, 3, 5, and 8.
2. Langdon Winner, *Autonomous Technology: Technics Out-of-Control as a Theme in Political Thought* (Cambridge, Mass.: MIT Press, 1977).
3. Compare Lewis Mumford's discussion of "etherialization" and "materialization" in *The Myth of the Machine*, esp. vol. 2, *The Pentagon of Power* (New York: Harcourt, Brace, Jovanovich, 1970).
4. See my "Obstacles on the Path to Organismic Ethics: Some Second Thoughts," *Environmental Ethics*, 11.3 (Fall 1989).

DISCUSSION

Joan Leclerc (Camden, Maine): Fred, in regard to what you said about Prof. Hellwig's use of the word "solidarity," could you perhaps have picked up more on the use of human will and choice? It seems to me that solidarity, in the way it was used, would involve a *choice* that perhaps the nonanthropic forms of life do not have available to them.

Ferré: Yes, that is correct. The question is well put; clearly, the relationship is not reciprocal between the human community and the rest of the biotic community, and the environment. That is why I never use the expression "animal rights." I think that type of language really is a misconstruction of the ethical situation. The ethical situation is that human beings have moral obligations to intrinsic value, wherever it is found. That puts obligations on us that are not, in fact, reciprocated by the rest of the universe, in any clear way that I can see. So, solidarity, in the sense that I'm using it, does not require a sense of receiving mutual rights from the other elements within the whole, with which, nonetheless, I believe, we need to affirm ourselves in moral solidarity. That is, I believe that we need to recognize the rest of the universe beyond the human community as moral *patients*, even if not as moral *agents*.

James Lindsay (Philosophy, Virginia Commonwealth University): I agree that to use the term "animal rights" is to put the problem in the wrong way, but I'm concerned that what you do in your answer is to perpetuate the tendency for us to take ourselves *out of* the evolutionary process, and become *observers* of the rest of nature, as if we were in some kind of privileged framework. I think perhaps, what we need to do is to *reinsert* ourselves into nature, and come at the problem Prof. Hellwig has raised in a little different manner, rather than to isolate ourselves from the rest of nature so neatly.

Ferré: I entirely agree that we need to take ourselves fully evolutionally, biologically (that's why I spoke in terms of what I called "personalistic organicism"). However, I think it would be unrealistic—and I would not be speaking what to my mind is the truth of the matter—if I didn't point out that there are repertoires available to the human species that are not available elsewhere. And among those repertoires are moral self-controls of various kinds. I don't want to be required to attribute those to the rest of nature in order to give it the respect of moral consideration that I believe it deserves. So, yes, if one can thread that difficult line between, on the one hand putting oneself hierarchically somehow apart from nature—because there are these repertoires that we have and we can't really find fully exemplified elsewhere—and on the other hand, recognizing our special obligations within the natural order, then we will have what we need in the new world of solidarity.

David Mog (National Academy of Science/National Research Council): It sounds to me like we are hearing some very strong statements that would encourage two things. One, that the religions of the world, and their leaders, begin to embrace science—and scientists and technologists—and to work with them. The other, that the major religions of the world begin to speak out very strongly about environmental ethics. I see little sign of either of these things happening at the level of leadership. Could you tell me what you know?

Hellwig: I cannot speak authoritatively for other traditions than my own. When I look at some of the religions of the world, it seems to me that they are more world-denying than world-affirming. But it is not for me to take that stand. If we are speaking of the leaders of the Christian communions, I think there are very hopeful signs. The American Catholic bishops, in their pastoral letter on nuclear disarmament (second draft), talked about the risk of destroying all creation as the greatest scandal of all. There was a great deal of ridicule in response to that, and yet I thought it was a very important comment. I see from time to time similar concerns coming from the World Council of Churches.

Arthur Peacocke: For thirty years the World Council of Churches has had a major program, in its "Church and Society" section, led originally by Paul Albrecht, in which an immense number of consultations with scientists and technologists were held. The WCC was represented in a major conference in Stockholm; they produced the great MIT conference of a few years ago. They have had a continuous effort to persuade the political world, and the ecclesiastical world, and the ordinary man or woman in the pew, of the need for just and participatory action, and for respect for the integrity of creation. That's one thing we have seen in the last three years, an immense and, I think, an extraordinarily fruitful, coming together of the five major religions of the world in connection with the protection of the environment of the species. This is the first time that the major religions of the world have found a common theme in which they can prepare to act together and exert pressure for the integrity of creation, and for human action on that problem. So the implication that churchmen do nothing is false. The churches have been screaming at the world to do something; church people are not responding very much, and the world is responding even less.

Ferré: That clearly is true; at the same time Matthew Fox, one of the most extraordinary voices on this question, is still silenced and I don't know whether that ban is going to be extended. There is uneven progress toward what needs to be done.

Mahootian: What sort of credibility do you give to an "earth religion," akin to pagan orientations, or to the alchemical orientation of the medieval times—of course modernized? In the light of what's been said in terms of the five major religions finding some unity on this single point, is there hope for movement toward a world religion beyond the religions we have had?

Hellwig: I'm not sure what an "earth religion" would be. Do you mean a nature religion? Historically, we seem to keep evolving away from that.

Ferré: I'm probably more sympathetic with the idea, but I'm sympathetic with it only within limits, because it seems to me that such organic forms of religion have historically had less than the kind of scrupulous attention to the needs of individuals, within the whole, than I would want to favor. That is, we see historically, these religions involve human sacrifice, and other practices that do not accord with my sense of what a "personalistic organicism" would need to have. So what I hope is that, in the greater ecumenical movement, many of the insights that are coming to the surface within our Christian consciousness (the same sort of thing that Arthur Peacocke was just talking about), which are also coming to the surface in Taoist and Buddhist and other parts of the world, could find different-perhaps even incompatible-mythic clothing from different traditions, but still speak to fundamental spiritual needs *within* cultural differentiation.

9

GENERAL DISCUSSION

Abridged and edited by Joseph E. Earley

Henry Williams (Cincinnati). There appears to be an insoluble conflict between what I heard from Professor Wilson and what I heard from Professor Yorke. After Professor Wilson's talk I went to him and asked "How does purposiveness, this tendency toward self-organization or self-assembly, arise?" Perhaps I pressed him too hard; he had no answer except "It arises because of greater complexity." Then I talked to Professor Yorke; his idea, from the mathematics of nonlinear dynamics, is that greater complexity brings chaos, instead of self-organization. To me this is contradictory—in one case, complexity brings integration and self-organization—in the other case, complexity brings chaos. Does anyone have a solution to that problem?

Arthur Peacocke. There is some confusion in the literature about this. Ilya Prigogine entitled his book *Order Out of Chaos* (Bantam, 1984); he was referring to some of the things I mentioned, dissipative systems for which, at a bifurcation, a new regime appears and the system oscillates between two states, or patterns of several sorts emerge. In these cases, orderly arrangements arise from less orderly ones. Now, these are things that we can understand in terms of the nonlinear dynamics of dissipative chemical and physical systems. But in some complex dynamic systems, such as those Professor Yorke has described in his recent papers, there are further possibilities—beyond the patterns that develop after the first bifurcation—such as chaotic behavior setting in. That is, chaos in the mathematical sense arises from an orderly state. Sometimes, beyond that, yet again, there are other transitions and some other kind of order occurs to replace the chaos. One had better be careful of slogans here, both sequences are possible—both chaos in the mathematical sense following what looks orderly and rhythmical and also the other way around. The book by Gleick (*Chaos*, Janson, 1988), includes very complex mathematical phase-space diagrams that make this clear. It isn't a matter of contradiction; whether order or chaos prevails in a particular case depends on the conditions.

Joseph Earley. If you have a nonlinear dynamic system—perhaps a very complex one—and you vary one parameter (the concentration of one component, say), at certain values of the parameter the system is stable and homogeneous. In some cases, if the parameter being changed grows larger than some critical value, oscillations occur—the system has moved into a new dynamic regime. (That is what the B-Z reaction does.) In the new regime it follows the same trajectory over and over again (it reaches a "limit cycle"). There is a *new structure* that has come into being far from equilibrium. Now, you may change the important parameter yet more; the prior structure may become unstable and then the system will diverge to something else. One aspect of Mr. Williams' question is: How do we know that there is a new structure beyond that one *from which* the system diverges? That, I submit, is a *theological* question. Whitehead developed the ancient notion that God is the *source* of integrations as yet unrealized. To relate this to what was discussed in the last sessions: Is there a way, as yet undiscovered, for humans to live together and maintain global equilibrium? The best answer might be "God knows!"

James Salmon, S.J. (Baltimore, Md.). As I recall, Prigogine talks about moving bifurcations, bifurcations after bifurcations and eventual return to chaos. Is it possible to reach an equilibrium that would remain indefinitely, after a bifurcation?

Peacocke. Some systems reach steady states that persist indefinitely but these are not true equilibrium states, since the system must be far from equilibrium.

Ernest Wolf-Gazo (Marburg, Germany). My impression is that what we have been doing for the last forty-eight hours refers to only a fraction of the world. Don't you think that what we have discussed only applies, basically, to Northern Europe and North America—not even Japan? I have been in Japan. Their technology is advanced but their social structure might be called "backward." Also, in the Slavic countries, where I have also lived, things look very different. We still are in the midst of the Enlightenment and the result of the Enlightenment is still not clear. It is a big experiment that has been going on two hundred years. What I would like to ask is, *to what extent do you consider that the rest of the world is part of what we talked about?* I assure you that I'm not convinced that the so-called progress of science will, at the end, win. I am not sure at all. That doesn't mean we will have religion all over again, like we did in the olden days, but I think something else will happen. I am not at all certain that the future will be similar to what we have talked about today.

Earley. We had hoped to make this meeting a joint Japanese-Western one, with the same topic. There is much to discuss about questions of individuality and cooperative action in Japan, and also in Eastern Europe and in Islam.

Frederick Ferré. Monika Hellwig had the Third World much in her mind when she was making her remarks about solidarity being a criterion for a proper Christianity.

Monika Hellwig. Whether we are inclusive or not depends on whether we are talking about people sharing the theory, or sharing the factual situation. Inescapably, everybody shares the same factual situation. As far as the understanding of it is concerned—and the discerning of values that are appropriate for our world—we can only work from *where we are*. We can only work out of *our own* roots. Even if we had an international conference and respectfully listened to what others have to say, even then we are not likely to come out of that conference with a *common* conclusion.

Participant. The results of discussions can reach further than common agreement on theory. If the effects of a change of thought in the West can result in a different economic policy that doesn't result in deforestation in Third-World nations, then—while the inhabitants of those nations may not pick up the change of thought—they will reap its benefits. The effects may reach further than the thought.

Robert Crosby (Washington Evolutionary Systems Society). I would like to offer an alternative view, one that is a lot less pleasant. The danger to the globe has been created by a relatively small number of powerful nations. It can be argues that those nations are primarily the ones who will have to change their ways—it may not matter what the others do.

Joan Leclerc (Camden, Maine). But there are many nations that you would probably not consider among the great and powerful ones that are stripping their rain forests. Many of the smaller nations of the Far East are despoiling their environments for reasons other than selling lumber to Japan. Look at the Laotian mountain culture, for example. They have systematically—over the centuries—stripped their mountains of forestation, in the same way the Greeks did in ancient times. Deserts are being created, not simply by power and greed in the West—or in some cases in the East— but by virtue of habits of life, followed over centuries by peoples (such as the Hmung) in countries that are not powerful.

Crosby. That is an important point, and it does reflect on what I say. What is behind my statement is that a huge Third-World economic development movement has been taking place since the end of World War II, sponsored by the developed countries. The impact of the developed world is absolutely global.

O.B. Hardison, Jr. I share the general opinion that this has been a highly informative conference. It has extended—in most surprising but enlightening ways—all the way from the arcana of computer simulations of chaos to the question of whether there isn't some "top-down" organization of the universe. I teach here at Georgetown, but this is the first time I have noticed that there is a phrase of Teilhard de Chardin inscribed over the entrance to this hall. I heard a lot of echoes of Teilhard de Chardin in the course of this discussion, which I found fascinating. I think this relates also to the notion that there may be a way that—even in their pluralities—the religions of the world may come together in some sort of unity.

I am suspicious of "solidarity." I have lived in this city for a long time and I think politics operates by interest groups. I think society operates best when interest groups take themselves seriously and passionately advance their concerns. I remind you that ecologists represent one powerful and articulate interest group.

Let me say, I was a little disturbed as the conference came to its end by what I thought was a kind of Luddite feeling in some of the comments, blaming technology for all the ills of the world. I was delighted that the question of the population explosion was raised. As you will remember, Paul Ehrlich raised that issue a long time ago, and it is still with us. It got to be unfashionable for a while but not it has popped up again, and we are worried. Well, technology has contributed to that problem, but it is a benign technology—called public health—which has vastly reduced infant mortality and reduced endemic diseases such as malaria, particularly in Third-World countries. Would we stand here in the name of solidarity and deny public health services to the Third World? I don't think we would at all. I do think there is also a benign technology which can contribute to the solution of the population explosion, particularly in Central and South America. But the lack of solidarity is only too apparent if I name it. It's called birth control. It's simple, it's benign, and I would guess some people in this audience would be very much in favor of it; some people would be very much opposed to it.

The church is very much concerned about social issues; we know that American Catholic bishops have signed a statement about atomic bombs and so forth, yet we know that the Catholic Church is not only opposed to birth control, but so opposed that they just finished firing Charlie Curran from Catholic University because, among other things, he was soft on birth control. So much for solidarity. I do not think it is technology that is entirely responsible for the ills we have been talking about.

William Sullivan. But you missed the main point that Professor Hellwig made; the point of the solidarity was solidarity in mutual autonomy, which means that *individuals* make decisions as to whether to use birth control. Was that not what you meant, Professor Hellwig?

Hellwig. I don't remember having said anything about birth control. But I did use solidarity in a sense I think different from Professor Hardison. My point was that the consummation of human freedom is inevitably a matter of cooperation and interdependence; that any model of human freedom that is set up in isolation is, in practice, proved false. Therefore we have to acknowledge at the outset that the possibilities of human creativity, autonomy, and freedom are dependent upon the relationships we are able to build among ourselves. The smaller the world becomes through communications, population explosion, scarcity of resources, and so on, the more urgent and the more widespread that interdependence becomes. When I spoke of solidarity I had in mind the acknowledgement of interdependence as a condition, not a prevention, of human freedom. Quite specifically, in the paper I mentioned that I am not talking about a *collective*, but a *communal*, realization. To me, those two words are very important because, given the conditions of the modern world, we all—not only the Russians, Cubans and Chinese—we all have the temptation to use high technology and powerful methods of control in such a way that a few people decide how everybody's life is to be conducted. To me that's collectivity. I'm not talking about collectivity, I'm talking about community. Community, of course, is the project that raises the really basic question—which I call theological—as to whether it's *possible*.

James Holly (U.S. Foreign Service, retired; Liberal Studies, Georgetown). I suggest that contemporary writers should substitute "universal" or "global" for "Western" wherever it occurs [in their writings], to test how their statements would apply to all four billion people [in the world]. The question [I raise] is: Must we have another global catastrophe such as [those] we had in this century in order to get at the issues that have been raised in this conference? If a conference like this had been held in 1913 concerning war, clearly, it would now be forgotten. What we remember are Verdun and the Versailles Conference; everyone here knows what happened to the Versailles agreements in 1942—and then there was Los Alamos [and Hiroshima]. In the year 2010 there will be eight billion people [in the world, and many opportunities for disasters like] Chernobyl and Bhopal and the *Exxon Valdez*, multiplied by an order of magnitude. Is it necessary to have such catastrophes in order to attain the sort of consciousness that the speakers at this conference are talking about? Is there some way to communicate the importance of this type of thinking to the four billion people of the world, before catastrophes happen?

Earley. I call attention to a mistake of the Shah of Iran. There was a contract for cooperation between Georgetown University and Ferdosi University in Mashad, Iran. (Mashad is the city of the founder of the Shiite branch of Islam.) A delegation from this University went to Mashad and was shown through the most sacred part of the principal Shiite shrine, in spite of the objections of the local people. The Shah ignored the mullahs. Conversely, Mashad has a large theological school; the mullahs there hear *nothing* about science. Neither modernity nor the mullahs will disappear soon. Both modernizers and traditionalists should consider the questions we have been discussing.

Louise Young. I want to go back to the first question, which dealt with the apparent confusion between the ideas of chaos and order. It seems to me that what we've been doing in recent years in science is assuming that chaos is the main factor in the cosmos; but since we can find examples of order, here and there, we have been trying to interpret these as small aberrations in chaos. Now, actually, it could be that we've got the thing backwards. It could be that there is a force in nature which is gradually building various complexities of order. Chaos also exists, but the chaos may be the waste—the leftovers—of these building projects. (I know I'm going against the regular paradigm, which is a very dangerous thing to do, but then I have traditionally done that sort of thing.) It seems to me that there is evidence that as time has gone by, things have become more and more elaborately organized and complex, and therefore more *capable* things have emerged. Which is the greater order or chaos? It depends on how you keep score. If you keep score just by adding up the number of disorganized things and the number of organized ones—then probably disorder would win. But, you might say, there is something we really have not yet learned to measure about order. We reach levels that are not really taken into consideration in applying the second law of thermodynamics. To give an example, you might take a group of letters of the alphabet and a poem of Keats, and ask how many letters are there in each. Yes, the letters in the poem are arranged in certain words, but a mere count would not give a random arrangement of letters any different weight than the arrangement of letters in a poem. It is very hard to put a *number* on the beauty of a poem, or on the rhythm, or on the meaning. We have not yet learned to take this kind of factor into consideration in estimating which is greater, chaos or order, and which is getting larger, and which getting smaller.

Participant (Herndon, Va.). There is greater and greater chaos in my mind—in the last two days I've acquired an intellectual hernia. Rather quickly, I'd like to vent my wrath on the last two speakers, Dr. Hellwig and Dr. Dupré, because they bear the brunt of the synthesis of all this. I believe in conservation; I don't like nuclear weapons. But then I'm reminded we have had bubonic plague, solar flares, the Ice Age, and the Great Flood mentioned in the Bible, the red tide, soldier ants and meteorites—but with all this, the planet is still here. I'm not so sure that we could destroy it even with nuclear weapons, although I hope we never try. My question is, if there is a purpose expressed in the world by the original source, then can arrogant man possibly think that he (or she) can countermand it?

Hellwig. Well, I just want to say, on behalf of the Creator, I apologize.

Michael Arbib. To deal with an intellectual hernia, we need an intellectual truss! An earlier comment suggested that the discussion here has been too Western-centered or perhaps too Christianity-centered. What I would like to suggest is that one can read what we've learned in the last day and a half as consistent with a non-Western, non-Christian, even atheistic, worldview. The first thing I want to note is the Professor Peacocke gave us a wonderful exposition of the emergence of order; how open systems could countermand the apparent dictates of the second law of thermodynamics; how we could start from very small structures and see more order appearing. And so we- finally arrive at the "chrysalis" of mankind. Now it seems to me that, if anything, that would suggest there was no God the Creator. The most one might hope for—shades of Chardin—is that the chrysalis of the human will lead to the emergence of God later. It may be that the physicalist worldview seen by some as support of a Christian worldview, is in fact *equally* supportive of an atheistic worldview.

A second point: I was struck by the fact that we only heard about evolution over immense courses of time. Although there was learned discourse about the Enlightenment, history played no real role in the discussion of what it is to be human. I thought the best example of this was when Olson and Margolis talked about how different backgrounds might make one give a case for monarchy or for democracy. Immediately, I was reminded of the fact that the present stability of democracy in Span was probably made possible only by the fact that there was a monarchy to protect it from the forces of reaction. And so—to think that there are somehow magical, universal principles that operate outside history is a mistake.

A third point (this may tie in with my comment on Professor Peacocke): Professor Dupré, after his beautiful exposition, commented during the question period that, although he wanted us to believe that he was a pious man, he felt that perhaps there was much work to be done before the time was ready for religion. If that is true, then the question is, if there will be a time for religion *what* will that religion be? Professor Hellwig gave us her Christian anthropology; she read the story of Genesis in a way that was to provide us with a rich meaning for making sense of the current world situation. Although Professor Ferré was very courteous in offering perhaps an extension or slight modification to what Professor Hellwig has said, I believe that he was showing us that the complexities of current technology make the story of Genesis an the Christian tradition irrelevant to the current world situation.

Finally, in response to Mrs. Young: As we trace the story of evolution, both in the physical realm and in biological evolution, yes, we do see the emergence of more complex systems. And, yes, it may be that what we are moving toward is a world order or cosmic order of some kind. But I think you should be very careful before you believe that is a *happy* thought. One of the basic things we know about organisms is that cell death is a crucial part of the developmental story of each organism. That means that even if we come to a cosmic order, there is no reason to believe it is incompatible with war and bloodshed, hatred and evil—on the level of individuals. On this happy note I close.

Louis Dupré. That was very nicely put. I would not presume to answer questions which I raise myself, and much as you do, and some of which, furthermore, are outside my competence. There are two issues that I thought were particularly interesting from my point of view and on which I would like share my ignorance with you. The first one is this: the new vision of the cosmos that is developing—the one that is emerging from modern science—is as compatible with the atheistic worldview as with a theistic worldview. I wholeheartedly agree with you, and I would add this—that even with the old worldview (I'm not speaking now of the Aristotelian system, because there you need a prime mover), once you are beyond Newton, then I think that any of these cosmologies are compatible with a religious or with a nonreligious worldview. This is confirmed, it seems to me, by the fact that none of those so-called arguments for the existence of God—if they are presented as real arguments, as proofs in the sense in which you and I understand a proof—is really compelling. They have been extremely unsuccessful. (I doubt that anybody has ever been converted to a religious worldview by an argument for the existence of God. I myself had never any doubts about God until I read an argument for Him.) So this should be conceded from the start.

The real nature of the religious worldview was marvelously indicated by the very last sentence of Professor Peacocke's paper, when he said: "*Who* loaded the dice?" This is a good question; it can never be more than a question. I think that religion is never a *conclusion* of any scientific worldview. It was once, for a while and to some extent, in the sense that the prime mover was an absolutely indispensable element in the whole cosmology of the ancient and medieval world, which in turn, led to the dramatic event of the modern age. That crisis was not due to the question of who is turning around whom—the earth around the sun or the sun around the earth. Copernicus dedicated his book to the pope; the pope was as pleased as Punch to receive it. In fact, he gave a very precious Greek manuscript to the person who brought [the book] to him. So, that's not the issue. The real issue was when that whole intellectual structure of the medieval worldview collapsed. That did not happen until Bruno and Galileo. At that moment religious people said, we need another cosmology if Aristotelian philosophy collapses, if there is a quasi-infinite universe. At that point, the phony support that science had been giving to religion—what I mean by "phony" is simply *nonauthentic* support—collapsed. So good riddance.

Professor Arbib's third point dealt with the question of whether the world is ready for religion. What I meant is this (I am a friend of religion—that is not the issue): I'm simply trying to say that a modern worldview (and I don't mean the scientific worldview in the first place or primarily; I mean the way in which we tend to identify reality with objectivity) is not conducive to any kind of serious transcendence. Anything that, in order to be real, has to go through my objectification process does not merit very much respect in terms of transcendence. That kind of God will, by necessity, be some kind of projection, and so will anything that comes out of it. In that sense, I was not arguing either for an abolition of religion in the name of the modern worldview, nor was I saying that such an abolition was really an impossible thing. I was simply saying that the preconditions are not such as to make a direct transition to transcendence possible in the way in which we usually state it. That means, specifically, that God-talk (specifically in the modern age—there was more of it in the seventeenth and eighteenth centuries than ever before) that talk is usually off. It is really speaking like the Sunday morning radio programs; God is good for this, good for that, and good for this other thing. Then you have a God who is really part of the world of finite beings. Of course, this kind of thing is intrinsically contradictory. I mean, not only hard to take, but contradictory for anybody who thinks about it for a moment. If God is infinite, is perfect, and all the things that we attribute to Him, then He cannot be an *objective* God because that would mean that He would be an all-inclusive reality. Ivor Leclerc and the Whiteheadians have worked that all out beautifully....

This is important not just speculatively and theoretically but above all, practically. God is something that fulfills, in Descartes' cosmology, a very particular function. Why would our American politicians—who never would think of praying—always insist on prayer in schools, breakfast prayers, prayer all over the place? Because its good for us. It's good for politics. This kind of nonsense is not going to stand up any longer—I quite agree with you.

George Farre (Philosophy, Georgetown). I wanted to comment on what Professor Hardison said earlier on the notion of community and solidarity between the First World and the rest of the world, the sort of isolation in which we find ourselves. Knowledge and technology are *cultural* products. To transfer such products out of one culture into another culture is likely to result in a great deal of turbulence, chaos. Not necessarily of the sort that is going to lead to a new order that is to be preferred to one that prevailed before. There *is* a culture gradient in the world, and that must be recognized if we are going to talk about solidarity, community, *or* collectivity.

Gary Ellsman (systems engineering, Washington, D.C.). Relative to a previous comment, I recall a pair of books, *The Coming Dark Age* and *The Promise of The Coming Dark Age*. The point of the second book was that when you are in a heap of trouble you need a big catastrophe for the system to reorganize itself. Intuitively, there is some appeal—a tragic appeal, perhaps—to the idea that very complex systems do need violent bifurcations if they are to reorganize themselves and adapt to changing conditions. I hope that's not true, but perhaps it is.

But I'd also like to ask a question. Professor Olson talked about accountability as a basis for government, and therefore as a basis for a lot of the cooperative and interdependent kinds of linkages that we're talking about here. It occurs to me that what many of the other speakers were also saying is that when you have complex and hierarchical systems there is a lack of causality between layers, possibly due to the chaotic nature of these systems. What we observe in our society, our democracy, is that government undertakes actions for which there is no effective accountability. One example is the interstate highway system, a system that has had decades of gestation, decades of implementation. Can we ever go back to the people in the 1930s and 1950s who started that program and make them accountable for it? Do we know what the results of that action were over the large span of time that a change in the network of that magnitude required? If our system is one that's that complex, and lacks causality between levels in the hierarchy, can we ever have accountability? Can we ever have effective interdependence so as to take purposeful social action to correct some of these problems?

Peacocke. With reference to the question we had at the beginning about the involvement of various other cultures: although the post-Enlightenment culture has shown various weaknesses and widening cracks, I don't think we want to knock the Enlightenment too hard. (I speak as an unreconstructed Englishman who wasn't involved in the founding of the United States of America.) But don't think we're ever going to go back to a stage where we no longer ask the questions "Why?—What are the reasons for?—What is the evidence for?—Is it coherent?—Is it consistent?—Will it hold up?—Does it hold water?" The Christian religion is the first major religion to go through this sieve. The critical analysis of its history, its Bible, its beliefs has been intensive, and still there are people, like me, who are pig-headed enough to follow the same course, even though the belief is altered in many ways. But even so, all the other major religions have not yet faced up to this critical questioning. The Enlightenment has yet to hit them—it will.

To respond to Michael Arbib's question about religion and whether the atheist's position is equally consistent with a lot of natural science. Yes, of course, that is the case. But the whole point is, what are you going to take as data? This comes back to whether his schema, either potentially or provisionally, is a serious attempt to depict reality. Now the schemas that we call religion, and what the humanities refer to, all the personal experience that constitutes the great humanistic traditions, including that of the religious experience over thousands of years, those schema purport to *refer to reality* under various names. They purport to depict reality—metaphorically, revisedly, yes—but that's what they are trying to do. So, if you ask the questions, "What makes most sense of all the data? What is the best inference for all the data? if the data *only* include what the natural sciences say at the moment, *yes*, you will get a position equally consistent with atheism or beliefs in an ultimate reality (in English, named God). But if you take into account a wider range of data, the data of the tragedy of human existence, of the experience of the divine in various contexts, the whole range of things—which I can't elaborate now—if your data are going to include that as well, and you ask yourself what makes the most coherent sense of all the data, then I think *that* is more consistent with theism than with atheism.

Theology student. My concern is that the divine imperative has been lost. People like Dr. Wilson have marvelously usurped traditional religious ground by saying that meaning is a wonderful mechanism evolution uses to keep us alive, that the imperative for finding meaning in our lives is not some divine goal, it is just a means to keep ourselves functioning. My concern is with the lack of any possible future direction. We have discussed the advantages of "getting our act together". The general reason why we should get our act together is to survive. We have considered various scenarios for what will happen if we do not succeed. The great world religions try to come up with revelations that explain *why* we should survive. I would appreciate any comments by speakers that are theistically inclined (or not so theistically inclined) to explain what part religion can play in society, beyond simply allowing us to survive—if indeed it has a role beyond that.

Dupré. I am theistically inclined. I would like to emphasize a point that was made earlier by Professor Peacocke. To say that a particular world cosmological system is compatible with this, that, or the other view (theistic, nontheistic, atheistic, panentheistic, pantheistic) is not saying anything against the viability of a religious worldview, or even against its indispensability. If I may put my cards on the table, I believe very strongly that without some sort of religious attitude, we will *not* survive. It's as simple as that. But that has nothing to do with whether a particular theology or worldview is compatible with a particular cosmology. The question is in a sense deeper. You referred to experience; this is exactly the point. As human beings, we should not take ourselves in abstraction, saying "Is this system compatible with that?" The question is—here we are, this is how we experience life, these are the needs we have to put things together.

I can see very well how this planet could survive with *none* of the present religions; as a believer I would have problems with that but I can see it happening very well. I would not make an argument against that. But I do not see how we could survive as *fully human beings* without any real (and by real I mean not just theoretical, but real) sense of transcendence. I think that without transcendence, you have no real freedom. You have something that inevitably leads to some kind of deterministic system. This is precisely the point.

We are in the Enlightenment, for better or for worse. There is no going back on the Enlightenment. Each time a traditional worldview is hit by the Enlightenment, by modernity, the change has been and will be *irreversible*, I'm convinced of that. Modernity is not the West. Hobbes said, about the state of nature, "In the beginning, all was America Well, we can say, "Modernity, at the end, will be the whole world." This kind of Enlightenment is felt and is experienced as being threatening. Islam, up in arms at this time, is an example. Why do they feel as they do? Because they fear that whatever we have to offer them is not worth the price. Until we have worked out our own confrontation with Enlightenment (which we have not done, I think), until we have worked out how we can preserve a genuine sense of transcendence, until then we are going to have problems with other nations when we introduce what we cannot but introduce, namely, modernity.

Thomas King, S.J. (Theology, Georgetown). Professor Hardison talks about human beings and machines living in a certain symbiosis. We talk of human beings and machines as two ends of a spectrum: on one end something that could be considered totally as machine, totally used for human purposes; at the other end the completely human being, never to be used as a means. It's almost as if there is a radical opposition, a Cartesian opposition if you will, between pure subject and pure object. I think this way of thinking can block our view, prevent us from seeing that, in some way, *we* are the universe come to consciousness, and therefore we are integral to the whole story. We need to realize that we are, in a sense, the incarnation spoken of; in some way we *are* the incarnation of the planet, and therefore we are not simply outside manipulators. This shows up in such issues as patenting life-forms, almost as if life-forms were simply machines. But we also must look for different categories to try to deal with such problems instead of just using a machine category. Maybe I should say we need some kind of sense of a "religion of the earth." Sometimes I feel very deeply in myself a religion of the earth, reaching out toward the Lord of Heaven and Earth. This, in some way involves my own feeling of being rooted into the earth, not being an alien form that could be objectified as a machine. It is out of that feeling that I find my own religious sense and orientation.

Frank Foreman (U.S. Department of Education). Economics has the distinction of being the first science of spontaneous order. *The Wealth of Nations* in 1776, the first major treatise of economics, discussed how individuals—acting on their own behalf—generate the order that we have in the economy. Adam Smith said, "It is not from the benevolence of the butcher, the baker or the brewer that we expect our dinner, but from their regard for their own self-interest." We have since found out that the economy doesn't run *simply* on the basis of people pursuing their own self-interest. We have found that "the self" is a rather ambiguous concept. We have learned that there are ethical presumptions and even religious presumptions to economic functioning, as Max Weber argued in *The Protestant Ethic* and *The Spirit of Capitalism*. The great lesson of the twentieth century is not the failure (or partial failure) of order to emerge from the bottom up, but the failure of order imposed from the top down. This century is a century of tremendous government failure. Early in this century, people believed in the notion of the omnicompetent state. Now more believe in the notion of the omni-incompetent state. The theme of this conference is the notion of community; it seems to me that government has destroyed the possibility for community. What actually has been fostered are pressure groups, which prevent community from emerging spontaneously. We should think more about the problem of planning; we may need to plan only lightly, only for small changes in underlying conditions that could generate better types of order.

Nelson Reppert (Center for Religion and Social Policy, Cornell). If we have concern for ecojustice, involving both ecology and the economy, we must be interested in how we're going to "get our act together. "Our act" is a phrase that has come up a number of times throughout this conference. The *primacy of praxis* is something I took for granted as I came here. I assume, maybe wrongly, that all of us are *involved*, and are going home to act in some way that makes a difference toward what is going on. Action, it seems to me, comes from within. We aren't acting from outside the situation; we find our responsibility for action within the organism (or the many organisms) of which we are a part.

Ivor Leclerc. There has been a considerable emphasis, justifiably, on the point that we're in the phase of knowledge which has been called the Enlightenment. It's been going on long enough for us literally to take it for granted. I want to suggest that we are right at the end of the Enlightenment, that enormous changes are occurring. We have been taking our science for granted and our ways of thinking for granted. Now enormous changes are taking place which will necessitate our rethinking, in a fundamental way, what we have been taking for granted in respect of our knowledge, and what constitutes knowledge. I tried to draw attention to one feature of this in my short paper. The work which requires to be done is one which necessitates the group of people who call themselves philosophers to be undertaking this task, because it is concerned with fundamental conceptions. I would like to say that my colleagues in this profession are far behind. They are not even beginning to catch up. There is a lot to be done in the decades ahead. That work will need to be done and integrated with, and interfused with, thought in the sciences, to make possible the rethinking of fundamental conceptions, which we *need* to rethink at the present time.

Farzad Mahootian (Philosophy and Chemistry, Georgetown). I want to thank Father King for saying what I wanted to say about "the religion of the earth" much more courageously than I would have been able to do. Regarding religion and science, I think it's not so much that religion can be based on science. Science and religion have co-evolved; when religion gets good, it is able to express itself more articulately in the language of a science which itself is more articulate. Religion draws strength from that; it draws the sort of universality that an earth religion, or a world religion, would need, by taking advantage of some of the changes in science. For instance, we need to realize the limitations of science, which are, in a sense, limitations of transcendence. The sciences of quantum mechanics first, and of the dynamics of open systems now, basically are indications of the limitations of science itself, or of the concepts of science. For instance, determinateness is limited, partly by our efforts to investigate nature. This sort of understanding is consistent with Professor Arbib's suggestion of various schemas floating around simultaneously; some go together and some don't. That is what the world is doing at every point, but especially now. There are various schemas (which I'd prefer to call metaphors or myths), that are operative in the world right now. I don't know if they can be all drawn together into one myth—probably not.

The Enlightenment purpose has been understanding *what* your own schema is, *that* your own schema *is* a schema and that it is limited; of understanding that other peoples' schemas are very important to them. If you want to communicate with them (while they still are in their benighted fundamentalism), you had better understand why they like their concepts so much, before you attempt to talk to them. That sort of understanding can be seen to be drawn straight out of the science of open systems. In this way science can serve as a source of a sort of religious experience.

Ferré. Let me just add a word or two about the dynamics of changing minds. It seems to me that religious traditions—real religious traditions, the historical ones that we are talking about as potentially being helpful or harmful to change—are very old, very traditional, very conservative formulations of fundamental values that have been, as it were, accreted over many generations, together with views of reality—as to what is considered ultimately important and what is considered real. They are fused together in ways that are very difficult to change; and yet they do change. Philosophers and scientists love to trumpet that they are doing new things—that nobody has ever really thought this before, and that everybody else is well behind them. We race, especially in the sciences, to have our manuscript in so it'll be received before anybody else can publish. That is very different from religious change. If there is a change, the religious person who presents it will say: "That's always been the faith. I'm not saying anything new. This is going back to the historical truth that has been covered up somehow—I'm just revealing it again." The psychology of change within the sciences and within religion are really antithetical to each other.

Now there is another way, outside the sciences and outside religion, in which there are value changes that do occur that may not be subsumable under either. (Perhaps that's where this religion of the earth that you have been talking about comes from.) There may be intuitions of fundamental ethical importance that are emerging in our time, not only in our culture but in many cultures—which are preceding the capacity of the traditional religions to respond. That doesn't mean that traditional religions won't respond, any more than they won't respond to new developments in the sciences. I think they will—they have in the past. We no longer believe in a geocentric picture of the universe. We no longer find it easy to accommodate Christianity with slavery. There are many ways in which we have changed, really and truly. I believe that this is happening now and that one of the things we must realize is that religions of the world have never had such an opportunity so well as today, under unique historical circumstances, to learn from one another; to abrade each other, but also to learn from one another.

I believe Christianity is handicapped, as I indicated in my comment, by excessive anthropocentrism. I think that is a deep handicap that Christians have to get over. They have to learn that there are other profoundly important values such as that of ecojustice that are not really easily incorporated into their traditional outlooks. Yet, when Christians do come to terms with this, they will say; "It was there all the time and they'll probably be right.

But Hinduism and Taoism and other forms of religion that are very important to us are also handicapped. They are handicapped by incapacity to recognize, without considerable change, the vastly significant importance of the individual, and of the natural order in which we find ourselves, and of the consequences of our actions. And so, they too will have to suffer in the ecumenical struggles that I see coming. I think both of these sides need to be kept in mind. We are in a very dynamic state.

William Sullivan. We have to underscore the *messiness* of the contemporary situation. At the same time we need to underscore the fact that we are not past the Enlightenment, but that in fact the Enlightenment is engulfing the planet, as Professor Peacocke suggested. I think that one of the crucial things that might be worth reflecting on is that ideas, or culture, don't float free (except perhaps in conferences such as this, or when intellectuals gather). To a great degree, culture operates through constructed ways of life and institutions. The way in which the Enlightenment is engulfing the planet is primarily through the larger structure that we call the world economy. Regardless of religion or culture, every society, every human being on the planet at this point, is affected by and must in some sense respond to the developing world economy. To cite one example, when we think of Islam and the problem of the Islamic refusal to meet the Enlightenment (to put it in a word, *Salman Rushdie*), what we see is that one of the reasons that Islam, for one hundred and fifty years, has never been able to make that move (although there has been a succession of progressive movements within Islam) was because, in each case, it was possible to beat back those forces on the grounds that they were the allies of Western imperialism, since the West has been the protagonist of these developments. It's clear that those developments are now quite beyond the West. But it would also be a mistake, on our part, to assume that we can very easily move to a situation similar to what was tried about a hundred years ago—a world congress of religions or a world congress of cultures—without taking into account that, in fact, all such meetings, all of this discourse, takes place in a *really structured* economic, political, institutional context. My plea is that if we are going to construct theological and cultural dialog, we try to put it in as realistic a sort of *institutional* context as we can.